ESCAPE TO THE

Riviera

To my friend John Mattill, who liked my work and inspired me to make it my career. Thanks, Owen

Photography by Owen Franken
Text by Nancy Coons

Fodor's

FODOR'S TRAVEL PUBLICATIONS

NEW YORK • TORONTO • LONDON • SYDNEY • AUCKLAND • WWW.FODORS.COM

Escape to the Riviera
COPYRIGHT © 2001 BY FODORS LLC
Photographs copyright © 2000 by Owen Franken
Fodor's is a registered trademark of Random House, Inc.

While every care has been taken to ensure the accuracy of the information in this guide, time brings change, and consequently, the publisher cannot accept responsibility for errors that may occur. Call ahead to verify prices and other information.

First Edition
ISBN 0-679-00787-3
ISSN 1533-5275

Special Sales

Fodor's Travel Publications are available at special discounts for bulk purchases for sales promotions or premiums. Special editions, including personalized covers, excerpts of existing guides, and corporate imprints, can be created in large quantities for special needs. For more information, contact your local bookseller or write to Special Markets, Fodor's Travel Publications, 280 Park Ave., New York, NY 10017. Inquiries from Canada should be directed to your local Canadian bookseller or sent to Random House of Canada, Ltd., Marketing Dept., 2775 Matheson Boulevard East, Mississauga, Ontario L4W 4P7. Inquiries from the United Kingdom should be sent to Fodor's Travel Publications, 20 Vauxhall Bridge Road, London, England SW1V 2SA.

PRINTED IN GERMANY
10 9 8 7 6 5 4 3 2 1

Library of Congress Cataloging-in-Publication Data available upon request.

Acknowledgments

From Owen Franken: Thank you again to Kemwel Holiday Autos for their new leased Peugeot, particularly Beatrice Geier and Melissa Alexander. Thank you also to friend Kathie Baccala at Qualex-Kodalux Processing labs, the photo-mailer people in Fairlawn, New Jersey, for the prompt and excellent processing of my many films, Kodak and Fuji. To Luc Fioretti and his terrific jeep in the Vallée des Merveilles, for his friendship, and his amazing knowledge of more than I ever thought there was to know about wildlife and prehistory. To Vittorio Falchi in Dolcedo for his camaraderie, laughter, and lessons in appreciation of really great olive oil. To Nancy Coons for introducing me to Café Turin in Nice (shellfish heaven) and to my patient wife, Annemiek, and kids, Manui and Tunui, for being willing to change hotels every three days so I could do my work. And to Fabrizio and Tigist for their excellent work in design and shepherding this through.

From Nancy Coons: Many thanks to Michel Faraut at Gôtes de France for hospitality and to Kemwel Holiday Autos for a zippy diesel Peugeot during the gas crisis. Thanks, also, to Valérie Pelligrino at the CDT Alpes-Maritimes, Marinella Mariotti at the La Spezia APT, and Elisabeth Lara in Cannes for quarterbacking. Thanks to Matteo Pasini at the Villa Steno in Monterosso for kind aid, both personal and professional. *Baci* to Vittorio Falchi and Lorenzo Trincheri for making us all feel at home in Dolcedo. Warm thanks to John and Alta for holding down the home fort. Loving gratitude to Mark, Elodie, and Alice for letting me escape to the Riviera. And homage and love to my footloose father, who inspires me, still, to hit the trail.

Credits

Creative Director and Series Editor: Fabrizio La Rocca
Editorial Director: Karen Cure
Art Director: Tigist Getachew

Editor: Christine Cipriani
Editorial Assistant: Dennis Sarlo
Production/Manufacturing: C.R. Bloodgood, Robert B. Shields
Maps: David Lindroth, Inc.

Introduction   7

La Dolce Vita   8
Hotel Splendido, Portofino, 92

Daughter of the Sea   12
St-Tropez, 81

Being Scott and Zelda   16
Hôtel du Cap–Eden Roc, Cap d'Antibes, 83

Green Gold   20
Olive Harvest and Pressing, Dolcedo,
Imperia, 91

The Mouse that Roared   24
Principato di Seborga, 90

Lust for Life   26
Tracing Picasso on the Côte d'Azur, 83

Having It All   28
Villa Ephrussi de Rothschild,
Saint-Jean-Cap-Ferrat, 86

Back to School   32
Ecole de Cuisine du Soleil de Roger Vergé,
Mougins, 84

Vineyard Vertigo   34
Grape Harvest, Groppo, Cinque Terre, 94

Que la Fête Commence!   38
Carnaval de Nice, 85

Importuning the Gods *42*
*Vallée des Merveilles, Parc National
du Mercantour, 86*

The Sounds of Silence *48*
Rocchetta Nervina, Imperia, 90

Red-Carpet Treatment *50*
*Festival International du Film,
Cannes, 82*

Le Grand Bleu *52*
*Research Expedition, Institut
Océanographique de Monaco, 88*

After the Last Boat Leaves *56*
Albergo da Giovanni, San Fruttuoso, 92

Inciting the Extraordinary *60*
Poets' Gulf, from Porto Venere to Tellaro, 94

Island Tête-à-Tête *64*
Mas du Langoustier, Ile de Porquerolles, 81

Backwater Visionaries *66*
Arrière Pays Niçoise / Nice Backcountry, 87

Glass-Slipper Time *70*
*Restaurant Louis XV, Hôtel de Paris,
Monte Carlo, Monaco, 89*

Five Lands on Two Feet *72*
The Coastal Trail, Cinque Terre, 93

All the Details *78*

Map of the Riviera *79-80*

Most books on the travel shelves are either long on the nitty-gritty and short on evocative photographs, or the other way around. We at Fodor's think the balance in this slim volume is just perfect, rather like the intersection of the most luscious magazine article and a sensible, down-to-earth guidebook. On the road, the pages at the end of the book are practically all you need. For the planning, roam through the color photographs up front: Each one reveals a key facet of one stunning section of the Riviera, conveying a sense of place that will take you there before you go. Every page opens up an exceptional Riviera experience; every spread highlights the spirit of this coast at its purest.

Out of one long stretch of Mediterranean blue the gods made two Rivieras—Italian and French—and here you'll get to know them both. What's your pleasure? You may yearn to strip down and sizzle on the hot sands of St-Tropez—or to jeep into the mountains in search of mystical rock carvings. You may dream of the steep green olive groves of Liguria—or of luxurious Belle Epoque villas and palm-shaded luxury hotels. You may seek out the festive throngs of Nice's Carnival—or ferry to the car-free island of Porquerolles. You may long to

boat straight into the Big Blue in search of whales off Monaco—or settle in for a three-hour, three-star feast in Monte Carlo. Or perfect your chopping technique at the Moulin de Mougins. Or ogle stars along Cannes's Croisette. Or hike the epic trail that links the five lands of Cinque Terre, high over the sea.

To capture the essence of both Rivieras, author Nancy Coons and photographer Owen Franken schlepped laptop and lenses onto ferries, jeeps, and yachts, rang doorbells to balconies over Cannes's red carpet, hiked Ligurian hills and Niçois mountain valleys, and lived on anchovies, olives, pesto, and espresso. But they never took this sun-blessed pocket of coastline for granted. "The exposure to so much gorgeousness," says Coons, "has spoiled me for life."

It has happened to centuries of travelers before her, and it will happen to you. So forget your projects and deadlines. And escape to the Riviera. You owe it to yourself.

—The Editors

THE LIGHTS OF PORTOFINO WINK FAR BELOW, GLINTING FROM YACHTS AND FISHING boats that bob hip-to-hip in the isolated harbor. A sfumato haze hangs over hillsides airbrushed with silver-blue olives, cypresses, and pines. Hanging over the bougainvillea-draped balustrade, you breathe deep the sultry scent of the good life. Like smoke tendrils from a good Havana, the ghost of Ava Gardner weaves elusively through the jasmine-scented dusk. This is the Hotel Splendido, Riviera playground of the jet set of another, more graceful era, and you are in quest of a suave, open-collared elegance lost to today's platinum-card buck-aneers. Your skin still hums from your late-day dip in the horizon-line pool; the aromatic-oil massage didn't hurt, either. Now, fresh from the marble-lined shower, you're ready for a late, summer-night dinner al fresco—course upon course of seafood trundled up from the port and sizzled in olive oil; a bottle of icy

La Dolce Vita

HOTEL SPLENDIDO, PORTOFINO

The view from the top: Balconies hang suspended over the tiny port, jasmine-scented breezes drifting down from the surrounding hills.

Pigato; an espresso so essential you dip in a finger and lick.... Sensuality and indulgence were the order of the day when Liz and Dick, Bogie and Bacall, Gable and Gardner, Bergman and Rossellini, and Deneuve and Mastroianni roared into Portofino in roadsters and sleek teak motorboats, a devil-may-care rat pack daring the sunrise over one last Negroni on the Splendido terrace. Portofino itself, a slender scoop in a tiny peninsula, its paint-box houses brushed in chalky pastels, was a film set for their real-life roles. A concierge once chartered a train to carry Barbara Hutton's baggage from here to St-Tropez, and a helicopter to scatter $50,000 worth of roses into the bay to assuage an Italian playboy's mistress. The stars still come, but they keep a lower profile: Streisand, De Niro, Ryan, and Quaid have all enjoyed creamy suites, geraniums draping over their port-view balconies. Half-board is de rigueur—where else would you eat, darling?—and daily bills hover around three million lire. But who's counting? Have another Negroni....

Feast on seafood just-off-the-boat and frolic in the horizon-edge pool, then wander down the path into Portofino for a stroll along the curving port lined with chic shops, yachting suppliers, and seductive *caffés*.

IN THE OLD PORT, MORNING SUN FLUSHES SHYLY ACROSS OCHER PASTELS, and pines and palms glisten with salty dew. Here, in her early-morning dishabille, lies the fishing port that Maupassant called "a charming, simple daughter of the sea." But as morning advances, daughterly demeanor gives way to provocative pose-and-pout. The first Vespa raspberries past, carrying a nymphette in platforms and hot pants; two black-swathed riders in nose rings squeeze a thundering Harley between leather thighs. Matching blonds with coordinated dogs and phones flop negligently into directors' chairs at Café Sennequier. Buff boys in little more than coconut oil emerge from gleaming yachts to swab the decks. Jade shutters swing wide and an old-town vamp, in five-o'clock shadow and scarlet-silk kimono, hangs a canary cage on the jasmine vine. And under the portal

Daughter of the Sea

ST-TROPEZ

A voluptuous, young Brigitte Bardot pouted on these sable sands, and launched a legend that perpetuates itself as an ambience of sun-and-be-seen.

of the Musée de l'Annonciade, a bottle-blonde granny, leathery brown in leopard-print capris, daubs a Day-Glo masterpiece. Lift your Vuarnets and check your watch: timing is everything, and you've played it cool. Show up at Le Gorille for your breakfast café-crème before 11 and you're a tourist for sure; head for Le Byblos before midnight and the bouncer screens you like a dung beetle, even with this month's Prada on your back. And tan lines—a *hint* of white on that perfectly bronzed cleavage or bicep and you might as well slink off to mortal Ste-Maxime. Feeling pale? Hop on your *moto* and zip down the route de Tahiti, where a cane jungle gives way to white sand and the blue horizon—the infamous Pampelonne beach. Bamboo bar-shacks pump head-shaking jazz, bold-stripe umbrellas skew with vivid abandon, and as far as the eye can see, bodies—breasts, bellies, buns—sizzle bronze and gold. Strip to the minimum, slather with oil, order a blue cocktail, and sink voluptuously into Riviera legend.

There's still the look of a Provençal
fishing port about old St-Tropez.
The picturesque backstreets are worth
exploring—if you can tear yourself
away from the yacht port, chic cafés,
and trendy, upscale boutiques.

Bobo cool: The bourgeois and bohemian live in stylish symbiosis here, where arts-and-crafts daubers stake out the waterfront and paint in the Vieux Port's famous light—reflected off gleaming white yachts.

MARRIED NEW MONEY? MADE A DOT-COM KILLING? YOU CAN'T take it with you, so you may as well Charleston while fortune smiles. When the Jazz Age literati adopted this grand hotel as their headquarters, they pulled out all the stops, and so should you: settling into the bachelor suite, snuggle that velvety robe around your chin, take another swig of breakfast champagne, put up your feet, and squint through your toes at the Arcadian perspective before you. Vast green grounds and an allée of pines and palms retreat symmetrically to Mediterranean blue. Bougainvillea hangs heavy above your basket of croissants, and the jasmine-sweet scent of pittosporum saturates the sultry air. Straw-hatted gardeners scuttle discreetly through the yew hedges; chambermaids roll a cart of linens silently away. Drain that glass of Dom. Enough

Being Scott and Zelda

HÔTEL DU CAP—EDEN ROC, CAP D'ANTIBES

This side of paradise: an exclusive playground for the wealthy ever since F. Scott Fitzgerald dallied by the cliff-edge swimming pool, the Eden Roc still pampers an A-list clientele.

lollygagging! It's time for a power decision: what will you wear to walk the long gravel path down to the Eden Roc terrace and the pool? This is *the* rendezvous of the stars. Yesterday you secretly toasted Michael and Catherine in the bar, and from your cane-screened cabana glimpsed Harrison behind his *Herald-Tribune*. Barbra kept a low profile under her parasol by the cliff-edge pool. You try to be cool, you try not to stare, but from behind your sunglasses you peer and hope. In another era, someone like you, in cloche hat or plus fours, fought the urge to gawk when Scott and Zelda jogged down for a swim, when Picasso made the waitress blush, when Hemingway ordered yet another Pernod. Then, as now, decadence, indulgence, and nouveau-riche extravagance were the order of the day... and when Fitzgerald set *Tender Is the Night* in the so-called Hôtel des Etrangers, everyone knew just which hotel it was. And still knows.

The price of privacy: Far from the madding crowd, cool cash buys you a screened waterfront cabana, a workout on the courts, and the *petits soins* of an army of discreet service staff.

IN THE GENTLE SILVER LIGHT OF THE LATE-AUTUMN AIR, THE HILLS ABOVE DOLCEDO shimmer softly under acres of delicate tulle, gossamer nets draped from one stone-walled terrace to the next, hovering like morning mist around the trunks of ancient olive trees. The feathery branches hang heavy with burnished fruit, and when you swing your slender whittled pole—*clack!*—a shower of olives and leaves rains down, bouncing like hail onto the net. Kneeling, Druid-like, you lift the bridal-veil edge and roll the olives into buckets, sieve out the leaves, then pour the clean fruit into thick burlap bags. Its bed stacked heavy with bulging sacks, a three-wheeled truck buzzes down the switchbacks to Dolcedo, where crateload after crateload rushes down a chute. Open the mill door and a cloud of oily steam rolls over you, bathing your face and nostrils in rich, fruity mist. Through the fog throbs the churning *ca-chunk* of the granite wheels turning inexorably

Green Gold

OLIVE HARVEST AND PRESSING, DOLCEDO, IMPERIA

Winter rites: The Ligurian hills don nylon veils to capture the heavy brown-black fruit— the *taggiasco* varietal—that will yield the region's distinctive oil.

through a massive basin of pulp—as they will turn daily through the winter. Workers sink muscled forearms into the black-brown mass and scoop it into hollow hemp *fiscoli,* then heave them into stacks on the vice-like press. Down the great screw sinks, squeezing, and from every pore oozes elixir. At the end of a Rube Goldberg sequence of pipes and pumps, a single spout gushes forth a thick stream of green gold, frothing, translucent. Stepping into the cold, clear air you stroll over arching medieval bridges, past the grand Baroque church built with olive fortunes, past the 17th-century stone measuring vats chiseled QUARTO DI OLIO. In his tiny shop lined with bijoux bottles of local delicacies, *oliandolo* Vittorio Falchi pumps bottles full, hand-caps them, and, with a roll of bright foil, seals them with a twist. *Ecco:* Extra-virgin, cold-pressed, unfiltered olive oil, the pride of Liguria, and in Dolcedo the stuff of life.

The hills of Dolcedo: Independent farms gather and process their own small harvests and carry them into local mills. The oils will be selected and blended by *oliandoli* for local consumption—or sales to international connoisseurs.

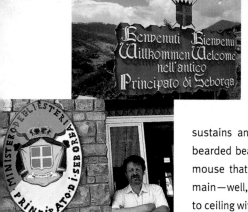

IT DOESN'T *LOOK* PRESUMPTUOUS. AS YOU WANDER THE TIDY COBBLED streets of this hill village above Bordighera, the word "unassuming" comes to mind. Yet miniscule Seborga, with all of 300 souls, might qualify for the all-Europe championship in chutzpah: claiming the title of principality, it sustains an independent constitutional monarchy. A portrait of Prince Giorgio I, a bearded bear of a man in dress whites, hangs, shrine-like, in every shop. Who is this mouse that roared? you ask yourself, contemplating the lions'-head fountain in the main—well, the only—town square. You step into a diminutive *alimentari*, stocked floor to ceiling with polenta, mops, figurines, rosaries, and movie mags; when you pay for your *limonata*, the aproned owner hands you a brochure—the history, she explains, of the *principato*. You settle onto a doorstep and immerse yourself in a parable of omission.

The Mouse that Roared

PRINCIPATO DI SEBORGA

Fortuitous oversight in the Middle Ages left tiny Seborga technically independent of Italy, and its modern citizens make the most of this in their own small way.

Seborga reigned as a powerful Cistercian city-state for centuries, then in 1729 was sold to Vittorio Amadeo II of Savoy. But wait: *Somebody forgot to write this down.* Nor was Seborga specifically mentioned in the 1748 Treaty of the Genoan Republic, nor in the 1815 expansion of the Kingdom of Sardinia, nor in the unification of 1861, not even in the reconfiguration of postwar Italy in 1946. Understandable oversights, some would say...but not Prince Giorgio I. In 1963 this publishing heir did his homework and proved Seborga's claim to the monarchy it first became in 1118. "Signor? Signora?" You snap back into the present. A wizened man is greeting you in semaphore Italian. "Entrare! Entrare! Aperto!" he urges, pointing down the street toward the palace doors. He pounds his chest proudly. "Io papa principe!" The prince's father! You step into the vaulted hall and, under another portrait of Giorgio, buy coins—locally minted *luigini*—bearing his noble profile. And, peering closely, you wonder: is that a tongue you see in the prince's cheek?

Lust for Life

TRACING PICASSO ON THE CÔTE D'AZUR

GIRD YOUR LOINS AND PLUNGE INTO THE HOT-BLOODED WORLD OF A MODERN MASTER. PABLO PICASSO lived or worked on the Riviera for more than five decades, and his presence still resonates through the backstreets of old Antibes, where he left a striking collection of work, and at Vallauris, where he left not only his work but his inspiration. At the Musée Picasso in Château Grimaldi, Antibes, vast masterpieces are mounted in the rooms where they were created, in view of the scenes that inspired them. Sea light floods canvas after canvas of satyrs and centaurs, mermaids and minotaurs; sun-faces beam ebulliently from platters, and jug goddesses present breasts and bellies bulging with promise. Something of a demigod himself, and just as potent, Picasso painted them in a heat of Mediterranean inspiration. Studying a still life of sea urchins, you catch a whiff of brine in the air and your stomach rumbles: reality check. Lunch, after all, was a consequential event in Picasso's day, as single-mindedly sensual a process as painting, sculpting, or molding clay. Or beachcombing with Dora at Juan-les-Pins. Or making love to

From Vallauris galleries to Antibes museums to the pétanque games at St-Paul-de-Vence, Picasso's vibrant spirit wanders still: sensualist, clown, iconoclast, bon vivant.

Jacqueline at La Californie. Or drinking red wine with Paul Eluard at Mougins. Or bathing with his children, naked, in Golfe-Juan's dawn-chilled sea. Through the streets of old Antibes the famous face stares, urgent, vital, laser-intense, from postcards, posters, and books. Accept the challenge in his eyes—head into the hills to the medieval village of Vallauris, where a pottery class carries on the tradition Picasso revived there. As you sink your fingers into spinning clay, you feel the wet Mediterranean mother-earth dissolving under your hands. Why do you still feel those eyes boring into you? At dusk you walk away spent and (is it fatigue?) spot a shadow of a man—a flash of bald pate, a striped *maillot*— disappearing in a dapple of plane trees. And for just a moment you believe: If ever a spirit could stare down Death, Picasso's could.

YOU WERE RIGHT TO WEAR LINEN TODAY. THE ART OF SWANNING THROUGH A roseraie and lounging negligently in a bamboo grove requires a Merchant Ivory wardrobe. The Villa Ephrussi is, after all, a kind of film set—one woman's fantasyland, an art-directed backdrop to a cinematic life. Like so many wealthy habitués of the fin-de-siècle Côte d'Azur, the Baroness de Rothschild knew what she wanted, and she wanted it all. First, a magnificent villa—Italianate, of course; pink would be nice. The house must frame a superlative collection of art and architectural details from around the world, from Renaissance grotesques to Baroque porcelain to 18th-century Chinese silks. It must command one of the most spectacular sites on the Riviera, the peninsula neck of Cap Ferrat, flanked with symmetrical Mediterranean views. And the grounds—ah, yes, how about theme gardens? Yes, seven would do, Japanese and

Having It All

VILLA EPHRUSSI DE ROTHSCHILD, SAINT-JEAN-CAP-FERRAT

A garden full of roses bearing her name, a house full of Renaissance treasures: the baroness spared no expense in creating her dream house above the sea.

Florentine and rustic Provençal and—why not?—the whole ensemble in the form of a transatlantic cruise ship, its deck a maze of geometric boxwood and fountains and blocks of roses, especially those hybrid teas called "Baronne E. de Rothschild." And we could dress up the gardeners as sailors in pom-pom berets.... Beatrice Rothschild spent a week or two each year in this cunning summer cottage, and you spend a day perusing her treasures: the Sèvres tea things on a bedstand tray, a snapshot of the baroness in pith helmet by the pyramids, her "necessary" travel kit from a cruise on the *Ile-de-France*. Saturated with opulence, retreat to your own humble villa up the beach, Hôtel Brise Marine. From the terrace of this more modest Italianate manor, the Mediterranean views are just as blue, the bougainvillea every bit as pink, the palm trees inch for inch as tall. Don your silk dressing gown, order a sweet vermouth, and succumb to delusions of grandeur.

Jutting like the prow of a boat high above the waters lapping the peninsula of Cap Ferrat, the Villa Ephrussi commands bisymmetrical sea views. Its seven exotic-theme gardens and its salons decked with Gobelin tapestries, Sèvres porcelain, and Renaissance grotesques are evidence of the baroness's creed: nothing but the best.

FROM THE TOP OF THE OLD TOWN, WITH GOLDEN SUNLIGHT DAPPLING through the greenery, you look out over the valley of olives and breathe in the scent of roasted garlic. This is the kingdom of chef Roger Vergé, who, from the landmark inn Moulin de Mougins, rules a hilltop dynasty of restaurants, boutiques, and a popular cooking school, all basking in the sun of the Côte d'Azur. In a tiny atelier atop this Provençal ziggurat, a handful of travelers sit scrunched into school desks, mesmerized. Behind the counter, the fast-forward blur of legerdemain—chopping, stirring, dousing with wine—pauses only briefly to answer a question before spinning away to check the oven and shake the sizzling *sauteuse*. Meet Serge Chollet, chef and heir apparent to Monsieur Vergé. Bantering in graceful Franglais, expounding on the evolution of French

Back to School

ECOLE DE CUISINE DU SOLEIL DE ROGER VERGÉ, MOUGINS

Recipe for success: fresh Provençal products, Riviera sophistication, inquisitive students, and a charming professor-chef create culinary magic, one step at a time.

cooking and the devolution of American eating habits, Chollet never stops for breath as his hands fly—"Le Paganini de la cuisine," he laughs. Or Baryshnikov, you think, as he dances from oven to range to blender and back, whisking a *beurre blanc* with hand on hip, whipping a blade through paper-thin onion slices without looking once, whirling to check the sea-bass terrines that puff golden-brown in the industrial oven. Charmed, entranced, his disciples for the day set down pen and paper and rise from their seats, some to peer into steaming pots, others simply lured, eyes closed, by the seductive aromas. At last forks are passed from desk to desk, and Chollet himself distributes the results of today's lesson: baby artichokes in a pool of herbed white wine; asparagus spears thrusting from a cloud of scrambled egg; a fan of sliced duck breast perfumed with lemon and honey. Silence falls across the room but for the reverent scraping of plates. Chollet lifts a beaded glass and beams: "A votre santé!"

WATCH YOUR STEP: THE ANCIENT TERRACED PATHS THAT BAND THE VINE-COVERED slope are barely as wide as your boot. Above you cant mist-bound green cliffs, below you a vertiginous drop to the sea. Set one foot before the other, adjusting the crate of juice-laden fruit balanced on your shoulders. Precious cargo, this: The tiny grape harvest of the ancient coastal vineyards of the Cinque Terre yield only a few thousand bottles of crisp white wine. For centuries the villagers of the isolated "five lands" of Cinque Terre have harvested thus, clinging like mountain goats to bluffs no wagon can reach—clipping golden clusters, then toting heavy baskets along precarious paths bolstered by hand-laid stone. In the old days they passed grapes in a rhythmic bucket-brigade down the hills to the sea, where fishing barques floated in the churning surf, ready to carry the fruit to the pressing. Today technology intercedes: Swiss-made monorails of shiny steel

Vineyard Vertigo

GRAPE HARVEST, GROPPO, CINQUE TERRE

Clinging to the cliffs, harvesters hand-cut sun-plumped fruit, then ship it down the near-vertical slopes to the Groppo Cooperativa.

carry crates by cogwheel to the road, where trucks rumble off to the Cooperativa Agricoltura. You ease your burden onto the tiny train and hitch a ride to Groppo, where another bucket brigade dumps sweet-scented fruit down a chute into a churning mass of pulp, already fermenting in its own juices. Breathing deep of the pungent musk, you wipe your brow with your bandana and head down to Riomaggiore. After the primeval hills, even this time-worn village seems to bustle with life, fishermen and farmers mingling with travelers. You stride down cobblestone streets to the thumb-wide port, where bright-hued fishing boats rock in the clean, sharp sea breeze. At a tiny terrace bar you settle in over an anchovy-smeared bruschetta and a bottle of Cinque Terre D.O.C. As brine and grape mingle on your tongue, they summon the words of contemporary poet Eugenio Montale: "In Cinque Terre one harvests fish and one fishes grapes."

Terraced in stone by ancient hands, these steep
slopes have been cultivated since classical
times, their grape crops basked in sea-reflected
sun and bathed in the dew of mountain mist.

WAVES CRASH ON THE FAMOUS PEBBLE BEACH, BUT TODAY THE WASH OF ANCIENT TIDES is drowned out by a cacophony of pounding rhythm, and Nice shames its subtle shades of ocher with an explosion of rainbow hues. It's Carnival time, when for 28 frenzied days the Niçois cut loose in one of Europe's most extravagant celebrations of pre-Lenten joie de vivre. Get into the spirit with the "flower battle," an interactive parade that puts the Rose Bowl to shame: float after float laden with lush bouquets rolls down the Promenade des Anglais, fantastically costumed beauty queens (and kings) hurling mimosa branches into the crowd. Between the floats flows pandemonium: bagpipes and flamenco, Florentine flag twirlers, Polynesian log drummers with flat bare feet undulating grass skirts. Commedia grotesques and Bosch-like specters jive and prance on stilts and unicycles. The driving drums—samba, salsa, disco, rap—pound in your blood and your hips sway,

Que la Fête Commence!

CARNAVAL DE NICE

Surreal: Dwarfing the mobs of revelers, gargantuan sculptures and the famous *grosses têtes*—literally, fat heads—fill the streets of Old Nice with fantasy.

unbidden, with the passing brouhaha. There are flowers in your hair, confetti down your collar, and you find yourself screaming alongside your neighbors, begging for another branch to complete your bouquet. And that's just the warm-up: tonight the floats are more elaborate still, a sky-high Carnival King and a gargantuan Queen, rank upon rank of larger-than-life *grosses têtes* marching down the street. Even the policemen spray strings of confetti, and the shaving cream flies. Suddenly, a shadow passes over the madness. Tonight is Mardi Gras, the last night, and the King awaits his doom at water's edge. As the crowd thickens quietly, a torchlight procession of hooded confrères winds to a halt before the giant. The streetlights dim in a moment of hair-raising silence. Then torch fire licks the king's hem, and with a *whoomp* he bursts into flame. "Oouuaahhh!" roars the crowd, as the mannequin, dragged with tow lines into the sea, floats, ablaze, and sinks into obscurity. And when you think nothing, nothing can top this spectacle, the fireworks begin....

For a month, King Carnival presides over a glorious world of pounding music, flying flowers, confetti, and shaving cream...until his immolation, marking the end of Mardi Gras and the beginning of dreary, sober Lent.

IT'S A LITTLE EARLY IN THE MORNING TO PLAY INDIANA JONES, BUT HEY—SWAT THE alarm clock, yank on your hiking boots, jump aboard the jeep, and shake hands with fellow travelers, archaeologists for a day. From the misty parking lot of Hôtel Terminus, St-Dalmas, you are about to crawl through the Valley of Hell into the Valley of Marvels. Your guide is already in four-wheel drive: Luc Fioretti, itinerant mountain man, expounds on history, botany, and mythology as he points the stiff-sprung 4 x 4 up a jagged rock trail, maneuvering switchbacks and plunging dropoffs with an insouciance you somehow don't share. Concentrate on the flora: pansies, gentians, rhododendrons, lilies, columbines, and blueberries carpet the forest hillside, lush in the early-summer morning. Just when your tailbone can't take another jolt, the jeep lurches to a halt in a broad valley bowl bristling with low scrub and ringed with dark-

Importuning the Gods
VALLÉE DES MERVEILLES, PARC NATIONAL DU MERCANTOUR

To enter the high, secluded Valley of Marvels you must hike or cling to a jeep trail, then climb steep, barren hills to find hidden treasure: mysterious Bronze Age engravings.

visaged mountains. Ease out and stretch—painfully—then follow your guide into the steep spill of boulders, climbing and clambering over slick stone, damp moss, and the trickle of crystalline springs. Luc tells of ancient fear cults, of mountain deities and celestial powers, of vindictive drought and lightning. What is it about this place? Mont Bégo looms over you, and the black clouds billowing over its peak send a chill through your Polartec and, lightly, up your spine. At last you see what you came for: a drawing chiseled in stone, a stick figure, manlike, arms raised skyward, toward the great mountain itself. In supplication? Curved bull's horns surround him: manly power? Impotence? A grid of squares maps one man's patch of fields: to guide the rain gods toward parched crops? As you walk, Luc talks: there are some 30,000 rock drawings in this Valley of Marvels, and though they've been roughly traced to the Bronze Age— around 1800 BC—no one really knows who carved them, or why.

No one knows why Mont Bégo inspired
fear and supplication, but some 40,000 rock
drawings seem to plead to its stony face.
For rain? Fertility? Shelter from fearsome
storms? Only the deities know.

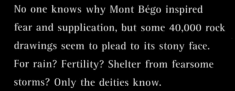

MAYBE IT WAS THE BEACH CROWDS, MAYBE IT WAS THE FORMULA 1 AUTOSTRADA driving, but today you felt you had to escape *from* the Riviera. At Ventimiglia you aim the car inland and wind into jungle-green hills—past farms, past a country inn, upward to the very end of the road. Rocchetta Nervina rises in a skew of stone cubes over a tumbling stream, two slender bridges forming fragile attachments to the modern age. You cross one cobbled arch...and step through the looking glass. Your steps echo as you enter a labyrinth of tall, skinny houses listing over guttered alleys, braced apart with slim arches as if by afterthought. A stone staircase, weeds bristling from its cracks like Rip Van Winkle's beard, hangs in midair from one withered-oak beam. A dragon's head drips monotonously in a dry fountain. A soft, clicking patter turns your head and a cat, wraithlike, dips under a cellar door. You have never heard a cat walk before.

The Sounds of Silence

ROCCHETTA NERVINA, IMPERIA

Time stands still in this ancient aerie, where a maze of alleys and passageways connects you to another age, and a mountain torrent roars between you and reality.

Where is everybody? A whisp of television music drifts through beaded fly curtains. When a church bell clangs you jump out of your skin, head toward the steeple, push open the old church door, and step into dim yellow light. Five gray heads face the crucifix, whispering. One rises, approaches a Virgin Mary in a halo of light bulbs, slips a 100-lire piece into the slot, and—ca-*chung*—an electric votive candle ignites. You slip quietly out, away, and back to the 21st century. On your way down the hill, you stop at that country inn, open the door, and are drowned in the festive din of a wedding, a baptism, and two first-communion dinners. A proud papa thrusts a glass of grappa into your hand, and before you know it you're waltzing to an accordian band. Even in Rocchetta Nervina, life goes on....

Red-Carpet Treatment

FESTIVAL INTERNATIONAL DU FILM, CANNES

EMERGING FROM THE PARKING DUNGEON OF THE CONCRETE FORTRESS CALLED PALAIS DES FESTIVALS, you blink in disbelief: La Croisette, the palm-shaded seaside promenade, has become a battle scene, and the Palace is under siege. Pointed white tents flank the promenade, guards in white-glove livery press back cordoned-off mobs, and broad-shouldered thugs in tuxes hover with walkie-talkies. In the grand hotels, publicists and paparazzi prowl restlessly, sandbagged behind piles of press kits. At last, a sleek autocade of Euro-discreet sedans snakes slowly through the crowd. There he is! Where? Who? A rupture in the ranks, and the mob presses in, thrusting faces and flattening palms against smoked glass. The car door swings wide and the shadows within emerge, Cinderella-splendid at 5 in the afternoon. A silk smoking jacket, a stiletto sandal, a whoosh of taffeta, and the red-carpet moment arrives: La Montée des Marches, the celebrated climb up the Palais stairs. A battery of flashbulbs, a cannonade of cameras open fire. Inside, another new film will be screened, flacked, mocked, and

A brush with the stars, a glimpse of the glamour, and a good time for all: you don't need to be a *cinéphile* to catch Cannes fever.

eulogized—the post-mortem parties hold the key. Champagne at Palm Beach with a live dance band? An intimate dinner for 50 at the Carlton's La Belle Otero? The port behind the Palais pounds with music: a red carpet stretches past yacht after yacht, each deck seething with a different social set. Looking good? A wink from the bouncer and you slip up the gangplank onto a gleaming white cruiser, *Titanic*-scale but threatening to founder under the swelling ranks of revelers, all warmed by today's carefully upgraded Côte d'Azur tan. Climb to the upper cabin, squeeze past the knot of bodies at the open bar, boogie past the frenzied dancers, and slip onto the deck, where velvety May air and peau-de-soie water sparkle with lights that silhouette the palm trees. Ah, yes—*this* is why they come to Cannes.

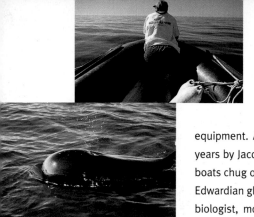

THE CONTRAST IS GRAPHIC. MONACO'S PORT GLEAMS WITH YACHTS, mansion-scale pleasure cruisers teeming with golden-boy crews. Dwarfed by the white leviathans, two patched Zodiacs—little more than inner tubes with sputtering Johnson outboards—sag with the weight of science equipment. A research team from the Oceanographic Institute, directed for some 30 years by Jacques Cousteau, is preparing a whale-study foray onto the open sea. As the boats chug out of the port, the Oceanography Museum towers above the water in all its Edwardian glory. Here Prince Albert I[er], Monaco's gentleman scientist and pioneer marine biologist, mounted the treasures of a lifetime's seafaring—exotic specimens in jars, bibelots in scrimshaw and mother-of-pearl, the colossal skeleton of a finback. And that's what you're after today: whales! Chopping across the azure water, clinging to hats, and

Le Grand Bleu

RESEARCH EXPEDITION, INSTITUT OCEANOGRAPHIQUE DE MONACO

As far as the eye can see, an undulating plane of azure conceals, then reveals, a watery civilization Jacques Cousteau called "the undersea world."

bending knees as shock absorbers, you cut a swath toward Corsica as Maurizio Würtz, the institute's *conservateur-scientifique,* studies a map of the ocean floor. With a canyon yawning a good mile beneath you, you stop abruptly to float in silence, and wait. Heads swivel, scoping the horizon, 360 degrees of unbroken blue. Will this be your lucky day? And then it comes: with a subliminal roar a stream of steam spews up, and a glossy black back rolls slowly through the surface. And rolls. And rolls. A male, some 78 feet long, Professor Würtz confirms, binoculars in hand. Then a female. And a calf. And, later, a school of dolphins leaping on their tails. And a sea tortoise kicking away, down, down, down. Cameras click, radios crackle, maps are marked, notes are scribbled. When it's time to head home, you're weak-kneed—partly from the waves, partly from sheer thrill. And when you stand at last on solid ground, looking out on the *grand large,* you sense with new knowledge its depth and dimension—indeed, the undersea world.

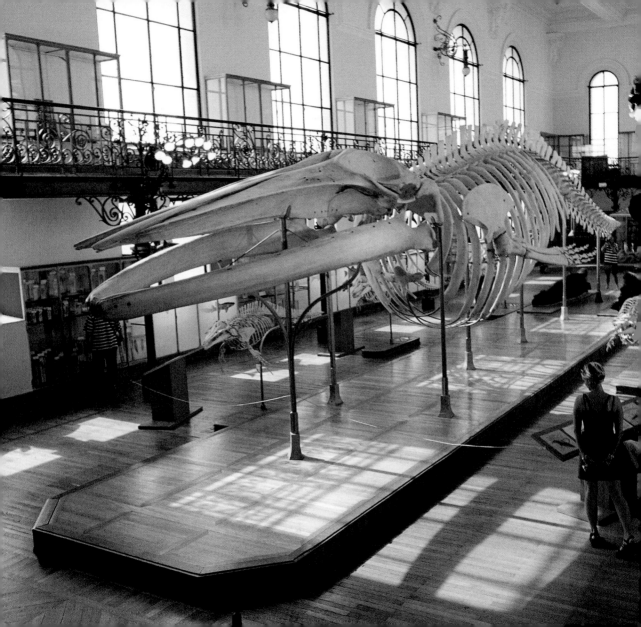

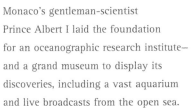

Monaco's gentleman-scientist
Prince Albert I laid the foundation
for an oceanographic research institute—
and a grand museum to display its
discoveries, including a vast aquarium
and live broadcasts from the open sea.

YOU CAN'T HELP FEELING SMUG. HERDS OF DAY-TRIPPERS FILE ONTO THE last ferry, sunburned, salt-caked, schlepping wet towels, abandoning San Fruttuoso and its ancient abbey at the end of a beach day. Yet here you stay, safely ensconced in the Albergo da Giovanni—showered, rested, and ready to reclaim paradise. Lean your elbows on the windowsill and wave as the boat totes its human cargo 'round the bend, the chugging of its engine giving way to the rhythmic wash of the waves. Below you, the beach attendants fold up rows of chairs, and taxi boats pick up the day staff and putt away. Upstairs, the clink of china sounds as the restaurant staff eats early, *en famille*; eventually the chef leans lazily out the window above you, smoking and staring at the bay. Saunter down to the beach and order a glass of Pigato under the Romanesque vaults of the abbey—earlier

After the Last Boat Leaves

ALBERGO DA GIOVANNI, SAN FRUTTUOSO

The monks who retreated to this hard-to-reach inlet found peace among forested cliffs and clear, rocky waters. One hotel now allows a lucky few to sleep over in monastic bliss.

today you traced its delicate cloisters and corridors, its tower and crypt. It's easy to see why Byzantine monks first sequestered themselves on this tiny hideaway bay. Climb the stone stairs to the restaurant balcony, where three tables are set: one for you, two for the rest of the guests. As you nibble onion focaccia, a fishing barque pulls up and a kitchen aide runs down to receive a tray of *gamberi*, their claws still waving; five minutes later they appear in your spaghetti *alla marinara*. After espresso, you lean over the rail and watch the water change from mercury to sterling to mother-of-pearl, the sky and sea merging into a platinum plane. Suddenly, over the forested cliffs that loom black above the bay, the rising moon, klieg-light bright, sends a swath of gold across the water. Tear yourself away to drowse under a shaft of radiance—and count your blessings till the morning ferry comes.

The tiny beach and a handful of bars and trattorias fill up by day, but you can sleep off each seafood feast in your simple room-with-a-view, then go for a night swim—alone.

SWING OPEN THE SHUTTERS AND TIP YOUR FACE EASTWARD OVER THE Golfo dei Poeti. The sunrise, soft as peach fuzz, refracts gently off sugared-almond facades as you lean out and gaze moodily across old Porto Venere. Brooding, are we? You aren't the first to run your fingers restlessly through unruly hair and size up the bay: two hundred years ago Lord Byron, fired by forbidden love, dove into these silky waters and swam an impulsive mile-long crawl to the home of his soul mates in Romantic rebellion, Percy and Mary Shelley. Tempted? Don't get carried away: Shelley drowned in these waves. Today, more practical than Romantic, you catch the next boat. Scudding over moiré waters, you spot the symmetrical porticoes of Villa Magni, San Terenzo, now flanked by beaches and commerce but then a windswept love nest. Shelley gave up wife and

Inciting the Extraordinary

POETS' GULF, FROM PORTO VENERE TO TELLARO

Epic landscapes, humble villages, churning waters, sensual breezes: The Romantic poets found resonance here for exalted ideas and earthy passions.

children to elope here with feminist Mary Wollstonecraft's 16-year-old daughter—while her stepsister carried on a liaison dangereuse with Lord Byron. From this hotbed of illicit love were born illegitimate children, torrid poems, and lofty ideals, fanned by the sensuality of the very Mediterranean breezes that now lick your skin. At the busy yacht port in Lerici, you disembark in the shadow of a 13th-century castle and, ignoring boutiques and cafés, catch a bus under the palm trees on the Piazza Garibaldi. Heading up toward the end-of-the-world fishing port of Tellaro, you're plunged into a painterly landscape of silver olives and coarse, twisted pines, with slivers of sapphire water glinting through the branches. D. H. Lawrence, too, found felonious bliss here, spiriting the wife of his language professor away to a beach-front villa in the red-rock cove at Fiascherino. *This* you can swim to—and, with a sense of symmetry, watch the sun set over Porto Venere.

Island Tête-à-Tête

MAS DU LANGOUSTIER, ILE DE PORQUEROLLES

YOUR CELL PHONE BLINKS "NO NETWORK." NO ONE CAN FIND THE TWO OF YOU HERE. PIRATES, Saracens, Moors, and Turks knew every inch of these waters off the coast of Hyères, but France Telecom has been successfully eluded. You've covered your tracks: you ditched the rental car at La Tour Fondue, hopped the *Star Méditerranée*, and crossed heaving waters to the tiny port on Porquerolles. From the docks, a vintage Dodge van carried you across the island, lurching over rutted dirt roads through eucalyptus forest, under shaded groves of parasol pines, past fig orchards, through vineyards. And here you are, on the terrace of the Mas du Langoustier, sipping the island's rare white wine and keeping the sunset to yourselves. And dinner al fresco to yourselves. And a cool, sleek room skewed toward the bay, to yourselves... Tomorrow, after an early round of tennis, you'll rent mountain bikes and explore the trails that lace cove after isolated cove, snaking through forests and lemon groves, then circle back to the

A nap to the rhythm of lapping waves, a bike ride through vineyards and eucalyptus groves, an intimate candlelight supper al fresco—all to yourselves.

Langoustier's arc of white sand and peel down for a swim in the turquoise sea. Later, you'll find a rock to call your own and play cards topless, wet sand oozing between your mingling toes. You'll indulge in a snooze in matching deck chairs under the pines, followed by a steamy shower in the room, followed by perhaps another *petite sieste*.... And then there'll be another glorious sunset, another dinner by the glow of a hurricane lamp, and a stroll under the rising moon. It was for just such a honeymoon that Belgian gold tycoon François-Joseph Fournier bought this lovely island for his bride in 1912, and her descendants, who run the hotel and cooperate with the national-park system, have preserved it for the finer things in life: privacy, luxury, natural beauty, and—sigh—romance.

COULD THIS BECOME AN OBSESSION? YOU START WITH A PILGRIMAGE up the Roya Valley to Notre-Dame-des-Fontaines, an unassuming 15th-century chapel in a forest glade. Behind the facade seethes a world of phantasmagoric visions, panel on frescoed panel from the life of Christ, painted with primal intensity. Crudely modeled, naive in perspective and expression, they must have struck straight to the medieval heart: a world-weary Jesus tormented by snub-nosed louts; Judus Iscariot hanged, a demon tearing his babelike soul from his bowels; the saved leaping, chastened, from a bone-filled tomb. Long before Web-cams, this is how the Word was spread: itinerant painters carried pigments and trowels from one backwoods commission to the next, telling a story with prime-time urgency. They penetrated villages still barely accessible today...and you do the same. Map in hand, you

Backwater Visionaries

ARRIÈRE PAYS NIÇOISE / NICE BACKCOUNTRY

Treasure hunt: Follow the map and borrow the key to discover, scattered through mountain villages, dazzling frescoed chapels painted in the 15th century by wandering Italian artists.

follow the back roads behind Nice, up the Tinée Valley, and down the Vésubie. At Clans, you're directed to a tiny grocery shop where chipper Marinette gives you a key and directions to the Chapelle St-Antoine. Sink the key into the old oak door, push—and gasp. A rigid symmetry of jewel-tone colors tells a story through the stains and mold: shadowed almond eyes, flat-poised hands, a Christ-vision floating in a cotton-candy cloud. Down the road, in the hilltop aerie of La Tour, tiptoe into the Chapelle des Pénitents Blancs, where workmen scrub centuries of candle soot from ocher robes and cheeks. In Venanson, high above St-Martin, pick up a coffee, a key, and a typewritten commentary in the village bar, then squeeze into the neighboring chapel to study the saga of St-Sébastien, super-martyr—shot with arrows, beaten with clubs, and stuffed head-first down a two-hole latrine: Not the stuff of downtown museums. You unfold your increasingly tattered map and continue your search for chapels and the backwoods world that produced them.

Horrors of death, joys of redemption: panel-by-panel narratives drive home the lessons of medieval Christianity, spreading the faith to the farthest corners of Savoy-ruled Nice. Giovanni Canavesio and his student Jean Baleison left epic works of powerful impact, rendered all the more vivid by local materials—ocher, schist, and copper—that have withstood the rigors of time and a harsh climate. Some have been treated to state-of-the-art restoration; others languish in damp, cobwebbed neglect.

Qd Iudas prolut xxx argentea i templo trahens laqueo se suspendit

clauar in cruce et dinumerata sut oia ossa eiq

DOMINI
PRESVTE
F...IO.
NEO.

STEPPING DOWN FROM YOUR PUMPKIN CARRIAGE—A MONACO taxi—you mount the Hôtel de Paris stairs as white-gloved doormen spin the polished revolving door. A blink, the wave of a wand, and abracadabra! Welcome to Cinderella-land. The lobby is a rococo riot of crystal, stained glass, and alabaster, a palace worthy of Prince Charming. Turn toward the restaurant Louis XV (that's Louis Quinze to the initiated) and, with a last pass at that stray forelock, step into the inner sanctum. Tail-coated footmen flank the entrance as you sink into celadon carpet, enveloped in a world beswagged in damask, glitter, and gilt. Your chair retreats subtly—yet another footman!—as you sink into your jacquard cushion, and a matching footstool appears at your side...just for your handbag. A caddy bristling with Champagne rolls up, and

Glass-Slipper Time

RESTAURANT LOUIS XV, HÔTEL DE PARIS, MONTE CARLO, MONACO

You could get used to this: Footmen at your beck and call, a crystal flute of bubbly, a panoply of culinary delights whisked from silver tray to golden charger.

you sip dry bubbly as a gilt menu slips into your free hand. Ah, yes: lunch! Not only is Louis XV among France's most extravagantly elegant and formal restaurants, it also happens to serve some of the country's finest food. Celebrity super-chef Alain Ducasse achieved the unprecedented when he earned the culinary world's highest ratings in two restaurants, Louis XV and his Paris flagship. On your golden charger there succeeds a series of sun-kissed chefs-d'oeuvre: truffle-sprinkled artichokes, scallops crisped in Ligurian olive oil, ember-grilled pigeon breast, salt-seared foie gras, hot wild strawberries on an icy mascarpone sorbet. Crystal stemware reflects white, then red, then gold as the wine is magically replenished after every sip. You select a gold-leaf-flecked chocolate from a porcelain egg and eye with smug satisfaction the Baroque wall clock, its hands stopped just before twelve. Have another petit four: as long as you sit here, you needn't go back to pumpkin-land.

MONTEROSSO SLEEPS BEHIND LOUVRED SHUTTERS, BUT YOU'VE SLIPPED INTO THE day's basics—swimsuit, boots—and are tramping down the cobbled street, a hunk of warm focaccia in your pack. Like the Ligurians who have peopled these coastal cliffs for centuries, you're off to hike the steep trail that once was their only link. Five villages on a string of promontories that undulate in shades of green and ocher, the Cinque Terre—five lands—still cultivate vineyards and olives on stony slopes that rear straight out of the sea. Only in the 20th century did the railroad connect the towns to civilization; before that, there was nothing here but the path under your feet and the fishbowl sky and sea. Climb rocky steps thick with brambles and spiny succulents, the air sharp with tonic eucalyptus. By the time you clear the crest you're already gasping—partly at the view. The whole broad swath of aqua sea spreads below,

Five Lands on Two Feet

THE COASTAL TRAIL, CINQUE TERRE

Sun and sea and a breathtaking cliff-edge trail link these five ancient villages, still car-free, though boats and trains add modern convenience.

slashed by snowy boat wakes, shadowed with schools of fish. And as far as you can see, knuckles of emerald land thrust into the water, the farthest obscured in morning haze. Onward! Emerging through Vernazza's labyrinth of pastel row houses, you strip and dabble your feet between fishing boats—red, blue, white—bobbing toylike in the tiny bay. At Corniglia, so high above the water that even boats can't land, you take in views from the ramparts, then clamber down the rocks for a swim and a lizard-wink of a nap on a sun-baked boulder. A precarious cliff trail threads into Manarola, where you idle in a *caffè* over the wave-washed rocks. By the time you reach the famous Via dell'Amore into Riomaggiore, the sun is already dipping behind the twisted pines. Couples sit, transfixed, on benches along the walkway, and you linger, hanging over the rail as the water waxes gold, apricot, rose. It's almost ferry time...and a five-hour hike has expanded into twelve.

The Cinque Terre paradox: Modern sunseekers mingle with traditional fishermen in village *caffès*, and hikers and farmers share the stony trail that snakes along the cliffs above an endless expanse of water. Artsy boutiques and hip focaccia take-outs cram shoulder to shoulder with *alimentari* and narrow row-house apartments, banners of laundry fluttering from their shuttered windows.

Painterly views: Every angle reveals another flawless composition, and the shifting sun tints soft mornings, vivid afternoons, evenings of silver and gold. Each village grows, organic, from the seaside cliffs, a Cubist skew of angles in chalky ocher tones.

All the Details

If this book whets your appetite for what F. Scott Fitzgerald described as "the diffused magic of the hot sweet South...the soft-pawed night and the ghostly wash of the Mediterranean," the following pages can take you there. These are the nuts and bolts of Riviera travel—how to get there, when to go, where to stay, whom to contact—plus some general information on the charms of each region.

Unless otherwise stated, all properties listed are open year-round, accept credit cards, and offer private bath. Prices reflect the full range within a category throughout the year (at press time, US $1 equaled 7.4 French francs, 2,184 Italian lire, and 1.13 euros). When addressing a letter, remember to add "France, " "Italy, " or "Principality of Monaco" to the address. When phoning or faxing France from the United States, dial 011–33 and then the number, *dropping* the initial zero. When phoning Monaco, start with 011–377 instead. For Italy, dial 011–39 and the number, *including* the initial zero. At sites off the beaten track, you may find that no one speaks English, in which case it's best to fax requests for information or reservations, phrased as simply as possible. The many Web sites listed here should also help with booking and background information.

If you're flying in, it's easy to connect directly to Nice or Genoa, usually from a Continental arrival point. Air France connects through Paris from departure points worldwide; KLM connects through Amsterdam from several Northwest Airlines gateways stateside. France's high-speed train, the TGV, will bring you to Nice from Paris in about 6 hours, but to really escape—that is, explore the backcountry and career along the coast—you'll want to rent a car from one of the major arrival points (St-Raphaël, Cannes, Nice, Monaco, Ventimiglia, Genoa, or La Spezia).

High summer on the Riviera—July and August—is overrun with sunseekers and the weather can be unbearably hot, even on the waterfront. Consider spring or fall to experience the mildest climate and café life in full swing. Die-hards swim in the Mediterranean all winter, hunkering against sun-warmed rocks, but most put off the plunge until May. The off season finds the majority of resort-area hotels closed and many restaurants, too; but those that remain open are full of locals, relaxing before the summer people arrive.

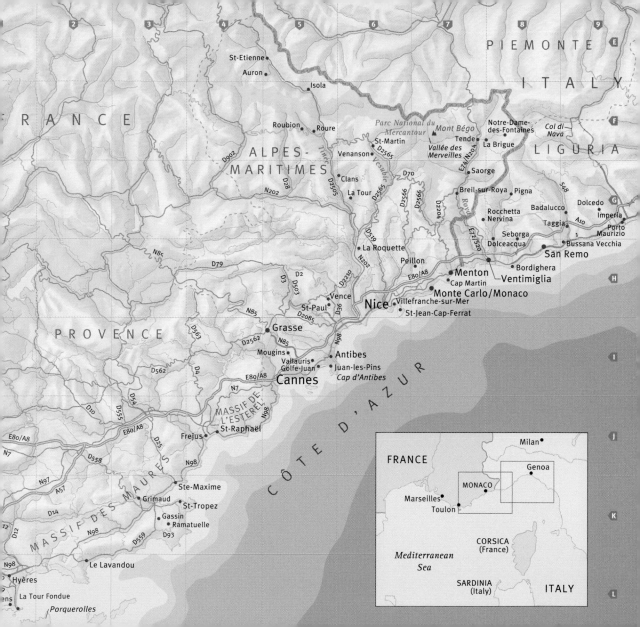

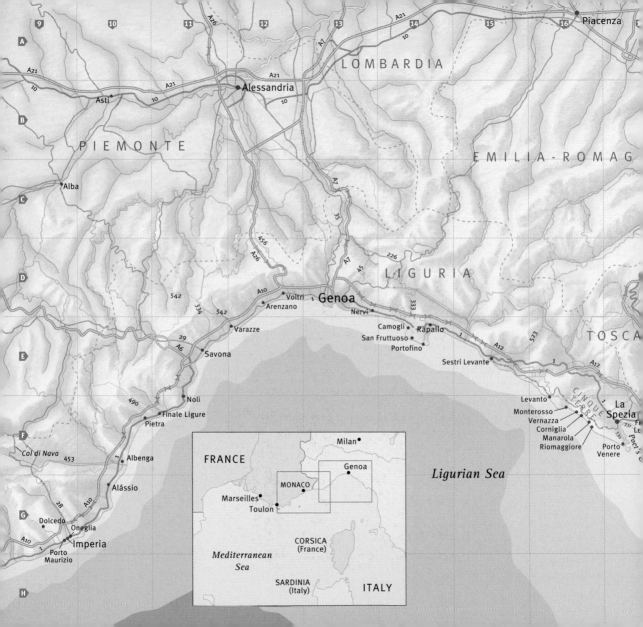

Grid coordinates, listed after town names in the following section, refer to the maps on pages 79 and 80.

THE WESTERN CÔTE D'AZUR

Just where does the Côte d'Azur really begin? Despite myriad beauty spots, the tough, sprawling cities of Marseilles and Toulon condemn much of the western coast to perhaps undeserved obscurity. But as you pan eastward from Hyères (1L) and its sun-coddled islands, palm trees replace Provençal plane trees and Mediterranean glamour kicks in. The procession of famous names that follows—St-Tropez, Cannes, Antibes (5I)—evokes turquoise waters, topless beaches, souklike *vieilles villes,* and the scent of fresh-caught fish sizzling in olive oil from the hills just behind. If you step back from the coast, even just a few miles, you'll find the classic perched villages of old Provence, rearing high over the coast where they once kept guard against invading Saracens.

ST-TROPEZ (3–4K)
Daughter of the Sea, p. 12

At face value, this modest little fishing port rarely lives up to its glitzy reputation. But like its Alpine counterpart St-Moritz, St-Tropez is defined by its people—the Right Sort of People, in turn defined not by bloodlines but by extravagant wealth, exuberant taste, and excessive good looks...and, of course, the wannabes that come to gawk at all three. It wasn't always thus. At the turn of the century, St-Tropez's ephemeral golden pastels challenged the palettes of Impressionists, with Signac, Matisse, and Bonnard all trying to capture the subtle beauty of the old port. But in 1959 filmmaker Roger Vadim walked into town with jailbait on his arm: the *pulpeuse* teenager Brigitte Bardot, who brought beads of sweat to the filmgoer's brow (*And God Created Woman*) and put St-Tropez on the modern map. There followed a stream of movie stars, leaving a wake of see-and-be-seen hedonism in beach clubs and discotheques that continues to this day.

CONTACT Office de Tourisme, Boîte Postale 218, 83994 St-Tropez Cedex, tel. 04—93—97—45—21, fax 04—94—97—82—66. www.nova.fr/saint-tropez. E-mail: tourisme@nova.fr

DISTANCES 66 km northeast of Toulon, 75 km southwest of Nice

LODGING Le Byblos: Reigning over the old town, the ocher villa-suites of this landmark luxury hotel are scattered around a pool and palm-studded court. Le Byblos is home to the famous Les Caves du Roy discotheque. Av. Paul Signac, BP 216, 83990 St-Tropez, tel. 04—94—56—68—00, fax 04—94—56—68—01. www.byblos.com. E-mail: saint-tropez@byblos.com. 52 rooms, 43 suites. 2 restaurants, piano bar, pool, massage, sauna, steam room, gym, dance club, beach shuttle. Doubles 1,580—3,950 frs. Closed April—mid-Oct. **Lou Cagnard:** Movie-star tastes and a wannabe budget? This small, familial hotel opens onto a tiny private courtyard, where you can breakfast under the fig tree. 18 av. Paul Roussel. 83990 St-Tropez, tel. 04—94—97—04—24, fax 04—94—97—09—44. 19 rooms. Breakfast room. Doubles 280—550 frs. Closed Nov.—late Dec.

OPTIONS The sole touristic must-see in St-Tropez is the Musée de l'Annonciade, a 14th-century chapel filled with Impressionist-era art, much of it painted locally. People-watch at the cafés along the quai Suffren and quai Jean-Jaurès, pretending not to stare at the Blessed Few on the yachts just opposite. Two blocks inland, the Place des Lices mixes Riviera chic with Provençal color under the plane trees. Wander and shop in the Old Town, a labyrinth of narrow backstreets between the Vieux Port and the 16th-century Citadelle that still lords it over the coast. The best beaches lie southeast of town, especially along the Plage de Pampelonne.

MAS DU LANGOUSTIER, ILE DE PORQUEROLLES (2L)
Island Tête-à-Tête, p. 64

What luck! Limited ferry connections and sparse lodging options keep this island-cum-national-park as secluded as an island should be. While day-trippers crowd the beaches and bike trails in high season, guests of the Mas du Langoustier have the priceless luxury of leisure...the time to take a sunset bike ride, a three-hour lunch, or a eucalyptus-scented dawn swim without keeping one eye on the ferry schedule. François-Joseph Fournier, having made a killing in Mexican gold, purchased this 1,200-hectare island in 1912 as a wedding gift for his bride Sylvia, then built her a hacienda and planted acres of fig trees and grapevines. Their children converted the house into a hotel in 1935, soon after which it was requisitioned by the Germans. Fearing further exploitation, the daughter divided the island between four heirs, then ceded three-quarters to the state as a national park. The quarter that remains in the family—still headed by the genteel matriarch, Lélia Le Ber—combines natural beauty, virtually untouched, with unpretentious luxury.

CONTACT Le Mas du Langoustier, 83400 Ile de Porquerolles, tel. 04—94—58—30—09, fax 04—94—58—36—02. www.langoustier.com. E-mail: langoustier@compuserve.com

DISTANCES 56 km southwest of St-Tropez, plus 20-minute ferry ride from la Tour-Fondue at tip of Presqu'île de Giens (south of Hyères)

FACILITIES 48 rooms, 3 suites. 2 restaurants, bar, 2 tennis courts, helicopter pad, rental mountain bikes, private beach on national-park land.

PRICES Half-board (obligatory) 1,298—1,577 frs. per person in double room; prices slightly lower May—June and Sept. Closed Oct.—late Apr.

OPTIONS Five-day Mas du Langoustier *forfaits* (packages) offer honeymooners considerable savings. If you're on a tight budget, opt for the pretty, Provençal-style **Auberge des Glycines,** directly on the village's eucalyptus-shaded square, open all year. Place d'Armes, 83400 Ile de Porquerolles, tel. 04—94—58—30—36, fax 04—94—58—35—22. www.porquerolles.net. E-mail: auberge.glycines@wanadoo.fr

CANNES FILM FESTIVAL (51)
Red-Carpet Treatment, p. 50

Make no mistake: Cannes's Festival International du Film is for cinema professionals with full accreditation, who attend screenings, conferences, shop-talk sessions, and, of course, parties by invitation only. But try telling that to the mobs in the streets, who hover for 12 days in this palm-studded resort town, hoping to rub shoulders with fame and fortune. If you are not a film-industry insider or a member of the paparazzi, do not despair: all the town's a soundstage, and the human drama is as much a spectacle as the stories on the silver screen. To maximize star-gazing, pick up a schedule for the daily *montée des marches,* when the cast of the featured film being screened—and all their friends—runs the press gauntlet up the red carpet into the Palais des Festivals. Stake out a spot near the limo arrival point to see the stars step into the crowd and make their ritual walk; dress up and stroll the yacht-lined port at dusk in hopes of crashing a party or two; or just content yourself with people-watching all along the Croisette and the Vieux Port, where scantily dressed starlets pout for the paparazzi and couples in formal wear sprint to make that private beach party. And if you put on a *smoking* (tuxedo) or the right little black dress, someone at the entrance to the Palais just might dangle a spare screening ticket under your nose....

CONTACT Association Française du Festival International du Film, 99 blvd. Malesherbes, 75008 Paris. www.festival-cannes.org

DISTANCES 30 km southwest of Nice airport, 69 km northeast of St-Tropez

LODGING Many of the biggest names hide out on the Cap d'Antibes at the Hôtel-du-Cap—Eden Roc (*see* Being Scott and Zelda, *below*). In Cannes, the triumverate of Croisette luxury palaces—the Carlton, the Majestic, and the Martinez—tends to be blockaded off for megastars, so consider settling in humbler lodgings nearby (though prices everywhere mysteriously swell come May). The **Splendid** faces the Old Port and offers palatial scale, if not luxury. Allées de la

Liberté (entrance at 4–6 rue Félix-Faure), 06407, tel. 04–97–06–22–22, fax 04–93–99–55–02. 64 rooms. Air-conditioning, kitchenettes. E-mail: hotel.splendid.cannes@wanadoo.fr. Doubles 730–1,430 frs. The **Molière** offers plush little rooms, most overlooking a vast tropical garden; book well in advance. 5 rue Molière, 06400, tel. 04–93–38–16–16, fax 04–93–68–29–57. 24 rooms. Closed mid-Nov.–end Dec. Doubles 460–700 frs.

OPTIONS Serious cinephiles can mingle with their peers at the festival even without full accreditation: Apply in advance for a badge granting access to screenings and conferences held in l'Espace Forum, a kind of vast (3,000-square-meter) industrial film fair at the base of the Palais des Festivals. A few last-minute day tickets are distributed to enthusiasts willing to queue up at the *acceuil* (welcome tent) in front of the tourist office, also at the Palais's base.

TRACING PICASSO ON THE CÔTE D'AZUR (5 l–J)
Lust for Life, p. 26

Through his long life Picasso called many Riviera towns home—Cannes, Antibes, Vallauris, Golfe-Juan, St-Paul, Mougins (5–I). But his influence—his presence, if you will—is felt most strongly at Antibes and Vallauris. In the latter, his *Man with Sheep* statue anchors the Place du Marché, surrounded every morning by the earthy street theater of the daily market; and in the Musée National Picasso on place de la Libération, Picasso's vast decorated chapel, painted with images of *La Guerre* (*War*) and *La Paix* (*Peace*), rivals *Guernica* for impact. Several ceramic works flank the entryway. To see more, visit the private Galérie Madoura, where the artist worked with his friends Georges and Suzanne Ramié; their son Alain still sells licensed reproductions of Picasso's work.

CONTACT Musée Picasso: Chateau Grimaldi, Antibes, tel. 04–92–90–54–20. Musée National Picasso: Place de la Libération, Vallauris, tel. 04–93–64–18–05. Galérie Madoura: av. Ramié, Vallauris, tel. 04–93–64–66–39.

DISTANCES: Antibes: 11 km northeast of Cannes, 15 km south-east of Nice. Vallauris: 6 km northeast of Cannes, 6 km west of Antibes

LODGING The greatest artists of the 20th century—including the ultimate bon vivant, Picasso himself—ate, drank, slept, and paid with paintings at **La Colombe d'Or,** in the village of St-Paul, 18 km west of Nice. These works and signed pho-tographs deck the walls of this stone-and-beam landmark restaurant and hotel, where you can dine on the fig-shaded terrace or swim past a Calder in the garden-bower pool. 06570 St-Paul, tel. 04–93–32–80–02, fax 04–93–32–77–78. www.la-colombe-dor.com. 26 rooms. Restaurant, bar, pool. Doubles 1,500–1,750 frs.

OPTIONS For a total-immersion Picasso experience, enroll in a summer ceramics workshop at the **Ecole Municipale des Beaux-Arts** (Espace Grandjean, blvd. des Deux Vallons, 06220 Vallauris, tel. 04–93–63–07–61). From July through September, you can opt for an intensive 30-hour week of ceramics practice (1,100 frs.); in winter, sessions last two hours or a full day.

HOTEL DU CAP–EDEN ROC, CAP D'ANTIBES (5–6I)
Being Scott and Zelda, p. 16

First opened in 1870, the Villa Soleil, as it was then called, joined forces and facilities with the neighboring Eden Roc tearoom in 1914, and expanded its luxuries to include a swimming pool blasted into seaside bedrock. After the Great War, two stylish American intellectuals, Sarah and Gerald Murphy, rented the entire complex and invited all their friends, a stellar lot: Hemingway, Picasso, the Windsors, Rudolph Valentino, Marlene Dietrich. Their most frequent and famous guests were Zelda and F. Scott Fitzgerald, the latter of whom based his thinly disguised Hôtel-des-Etrangers on this landmark in *Tender Is the Night*. Fin-de-siècle decadence and the winter Season gave way to democratic summer vacations, but Hôtel du Cap has always maintained an exclusive hold on its A-list clientele, and remains the lodging of choice for the Cannes Film Festival (*see* Red Carpet Treatment, p. 50)—don't even try to book in May. And if you're not a celebrity, tip heavily to keep the staff interested. Rooms in the main house are traditionally cossetted; rooms in the Eden Roc, right on the waterfront, are less interesting architecturally, but some have sheer-horizon sea views. The cane-screened private cabanas overlooking the water include changing room, shower, and Champagne bucket, and daily rents at least as high as those of the rooms.

CONTACT Hôtel du Cap—Eden Roc, blvd. Kennedy, B.P. 29, 06601 Antibes Cedex, tel. 04—93—61—39—01, fax 04—93—67—76—04. www.edenroc-hotel.fr. E-mail: ededroc-hotel@wanadoo.fr

FACILITIES 130 rooms. Restaurant, bar, cabanas, saltwater pool, massage, sauna, solarium, gym, 5 tennis courts, scuba diving, windsurfing, waterskiing, billiards, private yacht landing.

PRICES Doubles 2,050—6,500 frs. No credit cards (only wheelbarrows of cash).

OPTIONS Without leaving the Cap, you can sneak over to the even more luscious grounds of the **Jardin Thuret**, created by botanist Gustave Thuret in 1856. It was here that the first subtropical greenery was introduced to the Côte d'Azur, including the signature palm tree.

ECOLE DE CUISINE DU SOLEIL DE ROGER VERGÉ, MOUGINS (5I)
Back to School, p. 32

Under the direction of Roger Vergé, the Ecole de Cuisine du Soleil offers visitors *de passage* the chance to participate in Mediterranean cooking workshops without commiting the whole of their vacation. Classes last two-and-a-half hours and take place most weekdays year-round, some in the morning and some in the afternoon. You can sign up for one session, buy a *carnet* of five tickets, or arrange a private class for your group well in advance. Practicing professionals can enroll for even more sophisticated polishing sessions called *stages de perfectionnement*. Menus for each class are posted well in advance, so you can select those that appeal.

Serge Chollet, chef at the Moulin de Mougins, leads every session, switching easily from French to English.

CONTACT Ecole de Cuisine du Soleil de Roger Vergé, Restaurant l'Amandier, place du Commandant Lamy, 06250 Mougins-Village, tel. 04—93—75—35—70, fax 04—93—90—18—55

DISTANCES Mougins crowns a hill 4 km north of the Cannes city limit, 8 km from the Cannes waterfront.

LODGING In addition to its landmark restaurant, the **Moulin de Mougins** offers a few cozy-but-luxurious rooms in its main building and a few more-modern lodgings in the villa annex. 4 rooms, 3 suites. Doubles 880—900 frs.

OPTIONS Though you can only peek through a cane fence at his house now, Picasso (*see* Lust for Life, p. 26) spent the last years of his life in a sun-bathed hillside villa just southeast of Mougins, near the serene Lérins monastery, called Ermitage Notre-Dame-de-Vie. The setting itself inspires contemplation.

WESTERN CÔTE D'AZUR HIGHLIGHTS
The cork-forested **Massif des Maures** behind St-Tropez merits exploration by car for both its sunny rosé vineyards and its pretty perched villages, including Gassin, Ramatuelle, and Grimaud. Southwest of Cannes, the red-rock **Massif de l'Esterel** rears up over the sea, an evocatively barren scrubland covered with mimosas and wind-battered pines. At its base, pick up a map at the St-Raphaël (4J) tourist office to discover the best hikes both above and along the water. Despite its glamorous reputation, **Cannes** still presents a charming, if tiny, Old Town that spirals up over the sea, its morning market still drawing farmers from the surrounding countryside. In addition to the Picasso Museum, explore Antibes's quirky Old Town neighborhood, the self-declared Commune Libre du Safranier...then hike or drive around the lovely coastline of the **Cap d'Antibes**, taking in wraparound views from the lighthouse at its crest, called Phare de la Garoupe. Allow time to explore the hills behind the coast; northwest of Mougins, **Grasse** (5I) rises high above the coastline and features a triumvirate of highly tourable

perfume factories—Galimard, Fragonard, and Molinard—that make the most of the region's hothouse climate and the exotic flowers it nurtures. Grasse was the birthplace of the 18th-century artist Jean-Honoré Fragonard (1732—1806), whose family home is now a museum with paintings by Fragonard, his son, and his grandson (3 blvd. Fragonard, tel. 04—93—35—02—71).

THE EASTERN CÔTE D'AZUR

From the ancient city of Nice to the Italian border spans the most celebrated stretch of the French Riviera, sheltered from the mistral by high green cliffs, caressed by warm Mediterranean breezes, and backed by snowy Alps. The gentle climate coddles a veritable greenhouse of flora—roses, mimosas, jasmine, bougainvillea—and every waterfront promenade is defined by palm trees, first introduced at the turn of the 20th century. Beginning in the mid-19th century a stream of British and Russian aristocrats sought solace from winter chill along this waterfront, creating an exotic fantasyland of extravagant neo-Moroccan villas and tropical gardens. There followed robber barons, film stars, and restless literati who invented the all-body suntan and launched the unwonted fashion of summer beach vacations. The masses followed; today the coast bristles with pink villas skewed toward the sea, and its highways clog with traffic year-round. Yet the magnificent coastline, lovely harbors, and irreproachable views of azure water still survive. If the crowds press, head for the hills into Nice's *arrière-pays* (backcountry), untouched by Riviera glamour and as Italian in spirit as it is Provençal.

NICE CARNIVAL (6H)
Que la Fête Commence!, p. 38

Allied for some 500 years with the Italian House of Savoy as the independent county of Nice, this feisty, eccentric city has always had a will of its own—as well as a dialect, a cuisine, and a slightly louche political system. So when Nice decides to celebrate, it pulls out all the stops. The city commissions artists and composers, orchestrates wave upon wave of parades, hosts free open-air dance parties, and decorates the Place Massena with hundreds of thousands of flashing colored lights. The carnival tradition traces back to pre-Christian times, when the Romans fêted the arrival of spring. It was an easy transition for Christians to celebrate one last blowout before the self-imposed privations of Lent (the word *carnival* comes from *carne levare*, or "leave out the meat"). Throughout Carnival, the Old Town teems with revelers into the wee hours; the grand finale, Mardi Gras, brings several weeks' frenzy to a head. Rowdiness rarely exceeds the occasional ambush of spray streamers and shaving cream, so even small children join the party. To witness and/or participate, book lodgings well in advance, then pick up a calendar of events at the tourist office on the Promenade des Anglais.

CONTACT Office du Tourisme et des Congrès de Nice, B.P. 4079, 06302 Nice Cedex 04, tel. 04—92—14—48—14. General information: www.nice-coteazur.org. Just before Carnival, the tourist office launches a separate Web site for the event, named for this year's theme.

DISTANCES 32 km northeast of Cannes, 149 km northeast of Toulon

LODGING To be in the thick of things, book into the first-class **Hôtel Beau Rivage** on the edge of the Old Town, one block back from the Promenade des Anglais. 24 rue St-François-de-Paule, 06300 Nice, tel. 04—92—47—82—82, fax 04—92—47—82—83. www.new-hotel.com. E-mail: nicebeaurivage@new-hotel.com. 118 rooms. Restaurant, beach club, air-conditioning. Doubles 780—1,050 frs. To be near the thick of things but set back from the fray, book into the intimate, Provençal-chic **Hôtel Grimaldi**, 15 rue Grimaldi, 06000, tel. 04—93—16—00—24, fax 04—93—87—00—24. www.le-grimaldi.com. E-mail: zedde@le-grimaldi.com. 23 rooms. Bar, air-conditioning. Doubles 470—870 frs.

OPTIONS Both Matisse and Chagall loved Nice, and each bequeathed fabulous collections now displayed in the **Musée Matisse** in Cimiez (164 av. des Arènes-de-Cimiez)

and the **Musée du Message Biblique Marc-Chagall,** on a hilltop behind the train station (avenue du Dr-Ménard). On the place Garibaldi, the **Musée d'Art Moderne** features a vast collection of ultracontemporary sculpture and paintings.

VILLA EPHRUSSI DE ROTHSCHILD, ST-JEAN-CAP-FERRAT (6–7 H–I)
Having It All, p. 28

When the Baroness Ephrussi de Rothschild staked out her boat-shape turf high on the wrist of Cap Ferrat, she claimed one of the finest positions on the coast. Approached from Villefranche-sur-Mer, the road leading into St-Jean cuts sharply left and up a switchback—and into a small piece of paradise. Entrance to the villa includes the freedom to explore all seven of its theme gardens, from Japanese exotica to a solid bank of roses at the peninsula's "prow." Inside, a series of halls and salons displays an awe-inspiring collection of artworks, tapestries, and furniture, most of it Baroque or Italian Renaissance. For an additional fee, there are guided tours of the upstairs, where you'll see yet more Sèvres porcelain, more Chinoiserie, more rare French etchings—and a stunning balcony view that frames the boat-shape main garden. The glass-conservatory tearoom serves delicate lunches (tarts, quiches), pastries, and wine, and the gift shop provides a quick fix for the newly inspired gardener.

CONTACT Villa Ephrussi, av. Ephrussi, tel. 04–93–01–33–09. Access to ground floor and gardens 49 frs; guided tour upstairs 14 frs. extra. Open Feb.–June and Sept.–Nov., daily 10–6; July-Aug., daily 10–7; Nov.–Jan., weekdays 2–6, weekends 10–6.

DISTANCES 9 km east of Nice, 2 km south of Beaulieu

LODGING Hôtel Brise Marine ("Sea Breeze") offers small, homey rooms and a broad balustraded terrace high above the harbor. 58 av. Jean Mermoz, 06230, tel. 04–93–76–04–36, fax 04–93–76–11–49. www.hotelbrisemarine .com. E-mail: info@hotel-brisemarine.com. 16 rooms. Bar, air-conditioning. Closed Nov.–Jan. Doubles 730 –790 frs.

OPTIONS The small but upscale port village of **St-Jean** attracts a Docksider crowd, who park directly along the promenade to stock up, drink up, and dine on seafood at one of a long row of restaurants. Le Sloop is the most sought-after (Port de Plaisance, tel. 04–93–01–48–63). For walkers, the coastline promenade runs 11 km along the wave-swept coast, lush with tropical greenery.

VALLÉE DES MERVEILLES, PARC NATIONAL DU MERCANTOUR (7 F)
Importuning the Gods, p. 42

In the deep backcountry behind Nice and Monaco, cutting through Italy toward the Alps, the valley of the Roya River winds into the wild and isolated Mercantour National Park. Here, where gorges and pre-Alpine slopes are cultivated and grazed only under careful government control, the mountain villages have a marked Italian accent, and Tinker Toy train trestles weave in and out of steep rock cliffs. Only in 1947 did this region vote to rejoin France; Mussolini's hold on this once-Italian stronghold still stands in the form of a gargantuan neoclassical train station built in the miniscule backwater crossroads of St-Dalmas. High above the village of Tende (7F), accessible only on foot or by jeep, the secluded Vallée des Merveilles was home to a Bronze Age cult that worshipped and feared the deities of Mount Bégo. Some 30,000 drawings were chiseled into the broad, glacier-scattered stones that lie about, depicting tools, weapons, and fork-horned bull-gods, all traced to an era between 1700 and 1900 BC.

CONTACT To explore the valley on an all-day jeep-and-hike tour, contact Luc Fioretti, an accredited guide and driver (tel. 04–93–04–69–11). Maps, itineraries, taxis to departure points, and other guides are available through the Office de Tourisme de la Haute Roya, av. du 16 septembre 1947, 06430 Tende, tel. 04–93–04–73–71, fax 04–93–04–35–09.

DISTANCES Tende lies 45 km north of Ventimiglia (Italy), which is 30 minutes' drive east of Nice.

LODGING The **Hôtel Terminus** offers simple, comfortable rooms and good regional food as well as package tours into the *vallée* with Luc Fioretti. Across from train station, 06430 St-Dalmas-de-Tende, tel. 04-93-04-96-96, fax 04-93-04-96-97. 20 rooms, 16 with bath. Restaurant. Double room with dinner, breakfast, box lunch, and full-day jeep tour: 725 frs. per person. Double room for two nights with all meals and jeep trips to the Vallée des Merveilles and the adjoining Vallée de Fontanalba: 1,400 frs. per person.

OPTIONS The **Vallée de Fontanalba** is easier to reach on foot than the Merveilles and has some arguably prettier scenery. Jeep access allows more time to hike on site. Whether or not you make it up to the valleys, the superb little **Musée des Merveilles** in Tende is an absolute must—it illuminates the local Bronze Age culture with reproductions of the ancient drawings, samples of the tools they depict, and waxwork dioramas suggesting how people lived and worshiped in the Bronze Age (av. du 16 septembre 1947, 06430 Tende, tel. 04—93—04—32—50).

ARRIÈRE-PAYS NIÇOISE/NICE BACKCOUNTRY
Backwater Visionaries, p. 66

Behind the coastal resorts and the equally stellar hill towns that rise just beyond, the *arrière-pays* (backcountry) stretches all the way from the near-coast to the Alps. Scoured by harsh winds and thick with pines, scrub, and aromatic herbs, it's as far in spirit from the Riviera's palm-tree tropicana as it is from the North Pole. Villages are few and far between and often accessed by narrow switchback roads—so it's all the more astonishing to find this region peppered with tiny Renaissance chapels decorated with passion, intensity, and often eccentricity. Two 15th-century painters, perhaps of Ligurian origin, made the rounds: Giovanni Canavesio and his pupil Jean Baleison. Start your circuit by picking up the brochure "Seize siècles de patrimonie réligieux" ("Sixteen Centuries of Religious Heritage") from any regional tourist office and charting an itinerary. Up the Tinée Valley, northwest of Nice, you'll find the Chapelle Notre-Dame del Bosco at La Roquette-sur-Var (6H), the Chapelle des Pénitents Blancs in the hill town of La Tour (6G), and the Chapelle de St-Antoine at Clans (6G). If you press onward, look for the Chapelle St-Sébastien at Roubion (5F) and another at Roure (5F), the Chapelle St-Erige at Auron (5E), and the Chapelle St-Sébastien at Saint-Etienne-de-Tinée (5E). Circle east off the Tinée to see the Chapelle St-Sébastien in Venanson (6F), above St-Martin-Vésubie. For a quick fix, drive to Peillon (7H), behind Monaco, and look through the grille at Notre-Dame des Douleurs (Our Lady of Sorrows)...or content yourself with one pilgrimage up the Roya Valley (*see* Vallée des Merveilles, p. 42) and a drive through Breil-sur-Roya and La Brigue (7F) (both bristling with lush Baroque churches) to Notre-Dame des Fontaines (8F), where the most elaborate and hallucinogenic of all the painted chapels stands by a mountain stream at the end of the road.

CONTACT Mairie, La Tour: tel. 04—93—02—05—27. Mairie (town hall), Clans: tel. 04—93—02—90—08. Mairie, Venanson: tel. 04—93—03—23—05. Office de Tourisme, La Brigue (for Notre-Dame-des-Fontaines), tel. 04—93—04—36—07.

DISTANCES La Tour: 43 km north of Nice on D202. Clans: 43 km north of Nice on D2205. Venanson: 82 km north of Nice on D2565. Notre-Dame des Fontaines: 47 km north of Ventimiglia, Italy, via N204

LODGING At St-Dalmas in the Roya Valley (*see* Vallée des Merveilles, *above*), just west of Notre-Dame des Fontaines, **Le Prieuré** offers pristine modern rooms in a restored Romanesque priory. Rue Jean Médécin, 06430, tel. 04—93—04—75—70, fax 04—93—04—71—58. www.leprieure.org. E-mail: contact@leprieure.org. 24 rooms. Restaurant. Doubles 260—375 frs. If you undertake the Tinée Valley–Vésubie Valley circuit, consider spending a night in the scenic resort town of St-Martin-Vésubie (6F), where **Le Châtaigneraie** offers small, old-fashioned rooms in the main house and more spacious rooms in the new annex. 06450 St-Martin, tel. 04—93—03—21—22, fax 04—93—03—33—99. 35 rooms. Doubles 420—450 frs.

If you plan to explore the backcountry in depth, consider renting a home by the week from Gîtes-de-France Alpes-Maritimes, managers of a range of private properties including restored farmhouses in the pre-Alpine valleys where chapels hide. Depending on its comfort rating—2, 3 or 4 stars—a gîte can cost considerably less than a hotel room. For a catalogue contact Gîtes-de-France des Alpes-Maritimes, BP 1602, 06011 Nice Cedex 01, tel. 04—92—15—21—30, fax 04—93—86—01—06.

OPTIONS In the course of your painted-chapel crawl, you'll come across a boggling array of **Baroque churches,** many surprisingly large and ornate for their isolated small-town squares. No fewer than three flank the main square in La Brigue, including St-Martin, which contains a gorgeous polyptich by Niçois artist Louis Bréa.

If you plan to crawl around winding country roads (and Riviera highways) for at least 17 days, consider leasing a new Peugot from Kemwel Holiday Autos. Leased cars come with full insurance, unlimited mileage, and 24-hour emergency roadside assistance, and there's no VAT; you pick up your car at Nice's airport. For information call 800/678-0678 in the U.S. or consult www.kemwel.com.

EASTERN CÔTE D'AZUR HIGHLIGHTS
This celebrated stretch of the Côte d'Azur presents a parade of palm trees from Nice all the way to the Italian border, puncuated by postcard-perfect resorts like Villefranche, St-Jean-Cap-Ferrat, Cap Martin, and Menton, each with pleasure-boat ports and waterfront walks. Perched villages with a Provençal accent are never far away; Eze, for instance, rises sharply into the air from the coast east of Beaulieu. The best beaches—and full-service beach clubs—are in downtown Nice, off the Promenade des Anglais. If all that glamour (or high-season crowding) palls, head uphill and inland, where foothills and misty gorges wind up into the Alps. At Isola (5F), in the Tinée Valley, you can ski at 2,000 meters—within an hour's drive of the palm trees.

MONACO
Nestled on the waterfront between Nice and Menton, the Principality of Monaco is the seat of a feudal dynasty dating from the 11th century, and today boasts the most prosperous 473 acres in Europe. Its luxury high-rise apartments are manned by gloved doormen and served by purring limousines, and its Belle Epoque casino still epitomizes a James Bond sort of high-rolling cosmopolitan glamour. Host to the famous Grand Prix auto races and a prestigious tennis open, a flourishing ballet and opera scene, and one of the toniest yacht ports in France, Monaco rewards crowds of curious tourists with sheer novelty and a brush with medieval royalty, including a palace-court changing of the guard.

RESEARCH EXPEDITION, INSTITUT OCÉANOGRAPHIQUE DE MONACO (7H)
Le Grand Bleu, p. 52

People might look skeptical when you mention whale-watching off the Côte d'Azur, but Native American, Inuit, and early New England whaling traditions have long evoked vast, cold waters Continent-wide. Since 1995, this corner of the Mediterranean—from Toulon to Sardinia to Rome—has been a protected zone, a sanctuary for the finbacks, sperm whales, and orcas that roll in its depths in surprising numbers. The reserve severely limits the fishing and hunting that might upset the delicate ecology supporting these massive mammals, but at the same time it has spawned a new tourist industry: whale-watching. Long established as marine biologists in the waters off Monaco, the Institut Océanographique finds itself in a new role as whale-watchdog, observing the effects on the whales' way of life as man encroaches on their turf. Their research centers on the whales' habits—breeding and feeding grounds, familes and colonies, and reactions to boat motors, divers, and tourist paparazzi. In season, Institut teams make daily outings in two six-meter Zodiacs, heading up to 40 miles into the open sea. Serious sponsors of their research may accompany them on an outing; fans will soon be able to watch live broadcasts on screens in the museum, including underwater images.

CONTACT Mauricette Hintzy, Public Relations, Institut Océanographique, av. St-Martin, 98000 Monaco, tel. (377) 93—15—36—00. Potential sponsors—especially those willing to invest toward a new 9-meter hard-hull boat—should write directly to Maurizio Würtz, *conservateur scientifique.*

DISTANCES Monaco is 21 km east of Nice.

LODGING For the pleasure of hanging out on your personal balcony directly over the *grand bleu*, consider staying in the vast convention complex called the **Monte Carlo Grand Hotel** (formerly Loew's), 12 av. des Spélugues, 98000 Monaco, (377) 93—50—65—00, fax (377) 93—30—01—57. www.monaco.mc/granotel/. 619 rooms, 69 apartments. 3 restaurants, 1 bar, air-conditioning, pool, hot tub, health club, casino. Doubles 1,400—2,250 frs. If you'd rather donate that kind of money to the Institut Océanographique, stay at the humbler **Alexandra,** just above the casino (35 blvd. Princesse-Charlotte, 98000 Monaco, tel. (377) 93—50—63—13, fax (377) 92—16—06—48. 56 rooms. Air-conditioning. Doubles 700—890 frs.

OPTIONS In France, group whale-watch tours cruise the refuge starting at Port de la Santé, **Villefranche-sur-Mer** (6H); call the boat company, Promenade en Mer, at 04—93—76—65—65. On the Ligurian coast, the Corsaro leaves from the main docks at **Porto Maurizio-Imperia** (9G); make the required reservations at tel. (39) 0183/280110. The World Wildlife Federation collaborates with the Cooperative Battellieri del Porto di Genova to guide whale watches from the Pontile Marinetta from **Savona** (11E) and the Porto Antico in **Genoa** (13D); for information and reservations call (39) 010/265712.

RESTAURANT LOUIS XV, MONTE CARLO (7H)
Glass-Slipper Time, p. 70

Within the extravagant neo-Baroque Hôtel de Paris, cater-corner from the Monte Carlo casino, Restaurant Louis XV may occupy one of the most prestigious corners in Europe. Its kitchen placed in the gifted hands of Alain Ducasse in 1987, it quickly earned the maximum Michelin rating of 3 stars—and held them, phenomenally, when Ducasse won three more for his Paris venue in 1998. Despite losing a star in the meantime, Ducasse has gone global, opening versions of his trendy Spoon restaurants in London, Tokyo, and Mauritius as well as Paris, and a notoriously expensive eponymous place in the Essex House, New York. So who's cooking while Ducasse jets around the globe? In Louis XV, Franck Cerutti deftly executes the inventions of his chief (chef) while giving rein to his own culinary imagination.

CONTACT Louis XV, place du Casino, Monte Carlo, tel. (377) 92—16—30—01, fax (377) 92—16—69—21. Reservations essential.

PRICES The fixed-price lunch menu holds firm at 500 frs., but à la carte prices for a single course often beat that. Soups and salads average 300 frs., seafood 450 frs., meats 350 frs. In plumbing the depths of the wine list, plan to invest about a third of the total meal price.

LODGING The logical choice for high rollers is to check into a deep-carpeted room in **Hôtel de Paris** itself, the better to stumble upstairs and sleep off the feast (doubles 2,010—3,710 frs.), tel. (377) 92—16—30—00, fax (377) 92—16—38—50. www.montecarloresort. Alternatively, save your bankroll for the Louis XV and sleep 5 km up the hill in France, in the charming medieval hill town of Roquebrune. **Les Deux Frères** offers cozy, imaginatively decorated rooms and, from its good terrace restaurant, panoramic views over Monaco. Above D2254 in Roquebrune-Village, 06190, tel. 04—93—28—99—00, fax 04—93—28—99—10. www.hiv.nl/ deuxfreres. 10 rooms. Restaurant, bar. Doubles 545—595 frs.

OPTIONS The spiritual opposite of the Louis XV and somewhat more affordable, Ducasse's trendy **Bar & Boeuf** restaurant features a sleek Philippe Starck decor of glass, wood, and leather. Despite its name—sea bass and beef—its hip international menu is a long way from surf 'n' turf. Open in summer only at the clublike waterfront Sporting d'Eté, it opens out over the sea.

MONACO HIGHLIGHTS

The must-sees in Monaco are the **Musée Océanographique** (*see* Le Grand Bleu, p. 52) and the casino, where jacket and tie are required in the back rooms. Between June and October you can tour the royal apartments of the **Palais Princier**; then stop into the 19th-century neo-Romanesque **cathedral** to view the superb polyptich of St-Nicolas by 16th-century Niçois artist Louis Bréa, and perhaps lay a rose on the tomb of Princess Grace.

RIVIERA DI PONENTE

When you cross the French-Italian border between the Côte d'Azur and Liguria, the contrast between the two Rivieras is striking. Rows of shaggy eucalyptus perfume the air, laundry flutters from shuttered windows, hill towns conceal labyrinthine passageways called *caruggi*, and bright, wholesome cafés give equal display space to sparkling liquors and gift-wrapped candies. Welcome to the Riviera di Ponente, the cuff on Italy's boot, curving northeast toward Genoa—a stretch of ports and palm-lined beach resorts backed by dense green hills barely penetrated by modern roads. Its nickname, Riviera dei Fiori, harks back to days when the hills were carpeted with exotic flowers; nowadays the blooms flourish under plastic greenhouse panels that give the landscape a rather more futuristic look. Patchwork rows of every shade of green testify to the Ponente's new forte: commercially grown greenery that garnishes florists' bouquets, from eucalyptus to broom to ferns.

PRINCIPATO DI SEBORGA (8G–H)
The Mouse that Roared, p. 24

With 14 square kilometres and a population of 2,000, the cheeky little principality of Seborga was once a Cistercian city-state of some consequence, ruled by an elected prince-abbot for 600 years. Under the aegis of St. Bernard of Clairvaux, Seborga sent nine Knights Templar to Jerusalem to fight the infidels, and all nine returned to be consecrated by St.

Bernard himself. Not much has happened in Seborga since then; it's a sleepy little hill town of twisting alleyways and vaulted *caruggi*, with a handful of shops and three restaurant-cafés...and the latter owe their existence to the influx of curious visitors who wander the streets, peek into the Baroque church, and buy souvenirs: stamps bearing Prince Giorgio's profile and *luigini*, the local currency. Seborga is at its best during the *festini*—Thursday and Saturday nights in July and August—when local families set up tables and benches on the streets and serve home-cooked local specialties, especially goat and rabbit.

CONTACT Seborga tourist office, Palazzo del Governo, via della Zecca 7, tel. 0184/223924.

DISTANCES Seborga lies 10 km northeast of Bordighera. Directions from both the autostrada (Exit 146 at Bordighera) and the coastal highway SS1 are well marked.

LODGING The principality being too small to support a hotel, travelers can spend the night in the gracious seaside resort of Bordighera, 10 km below Seborga. **Hotel Piccolo Lido** offers a sun terrace and direct beach access, and half the rooms have sea-view balconies. Lungomare Argentina 2, 18012 Bordighera, Imperia, tel. 0184/261297, fax 0184/262316. www.hplido.masterweb.it. E-mail: hplido@masterweb.it. Restaurant, bar, air-conditioning. Doubles 145,000—240,000 lire.

OPTIONS Visit **Bordighera**'s (8H) hillside Old Town, ogle its neo-Gothic fin-de-siècle mansions, and—with your jacket draped over your shoulders, of course—stroll down the waterfront promenade called Lungomare Argentina.

ROCCHETTA NERVINA, IMPERIA (7–8G)
The Sounds of Silence, p. 48

At the very end of a winding road 12 km north of Ventimiglia (8H)—and thus undisturbed by through traffic—Rocchetta Nervina maintains a Brigadoon air, frozen in time, floating ethereally above the Barbaira Valley it once protected under the name Castrum Barbaira. Hikers might consider it home base for forays into the green wilds around it, including

Monte Morgi (819 m) and Monte Terca (1,070 m).

DISTANCES 12 km north of Ventimiglia via Dolceacqua (head left at Ponte Barbaira and drive till the road runs out)

LODGING Hotel Lago Bin is a local institution, founded by a patriarch who filled it with family and hunting trophies. It's now run by his widow, Grandma Marguerita—who first covered the tables with her own wedding linens and now, at 77, mans the kitchen—and by their children and grandchildren. The vast facilities encourage wedding, baptism, and pool parties, but doilies and stuffed wild boar sustain the mountain-inn ambience. 18035 Rocchetta Nervina, Imperia, tel. 0184/207108, fax 0184/207827. www.lagobin.com. E-mail lagobinlagobin.com. 60 rooms. Restaurant, bar, pool, tennis court. Doubles 150,000—190,000 lire.

OPTIONS Halfway between Rocchetta and Ventimiglia, **Dolceacqua** (8H) is an ancient medieval stronghold that straddles the Nervia River. Its castle, built by the ruling Doria family, dominates the Old Town, which is joined to the modern quarter via a slender, multivaulted bridge dating from the Middle Ages. In Sant'Antonio Abate (part church, part defensive tower), look for the polyptich of St-Devota by Niçois artist Louis Bréa.

OLIVE HARVEST AND PRESSING, DOLCEDO, IMPERIA (9G)
Green Gold, p. 20

At the heart of olive production since Roman times, Imperia and its inland anchor, Dolcedo, were struck by a killer frost in the Middle Ages—good luck, as it turned out. Benedictine monks replanted using frost-resistant *taggiasca* olive trees imported from Palestine, and established a single-varietal olive industry that thrives to this day. The characteristic taggiasca olives can ripen anytime between November and April; a late-harvest pressing yields the mildest, sweetest *biancardo* oil. Around this culture of fine Imperia oils flourishes a cottage industry of *prodotti tipici,* a series of sauces, condiments, and antipasti all based on the region's fine oil.

CONTACT In Dolcedo's miniature center, expert *oliandolo* Vit-

torio Falchi sells a line of his own products as well as the oil he tastes, selects, and blends for a consistent product, all under the label Pietrantica (Piazza Doria, 40, 18024 Dolcedo, tel. 0183/281008, fax 0183/281849. In the hills near Lecchiore, the Ranise family presses and bottles its own line of home-grown oil as well as prodotti tipici, including a fresh-tasting oil pressed with lemon peel. Via IV Novembre 29, Dolcedo-Lecchiore, Imperia, tel. 0183/291615, fax 0183/295129.

DISTANCES Dolcedo lies 10 km inland from Imperia; look for signs just west of the Imperia Ovest exit from the A10.

LODGING As there are no hotels as yet in little Dolcedo, consider renting an **agriturismo** (farm-based vacation apartment). There are nine in the hamlets clustered in the hills nearby, many on olive-producing properties. On a larger scale, there's no shortage of **private villas** for rent, many in restored stone houses. Contact Lorenzo Trincheri, Immobiliare Valprino, Piazza Doria 26, 18024 Dolcedo, Imperia, tel./fax 0183/280140. Email: valprino@uno.it. For a classic hotel stopover, head back to the coast (10 km) to Porto Maurizio. (Porto Maurizio's eastern twin city, Oneglia, is the industrial capital of both olive oil and pasta.) The **Hotel Croce de Malta,** 50 m from the waves in the heart of Porto Maurizio's busy beach scene, offers 39 rooms, nearly all with sea views. Via Scarincio 148, 18100 Imperia, tel. 0183/667020, fax 0183/63687. www.hotelcrocedimalta.com. E-mail: info@hotelcrocedimalta.com. Restaurant, private beach. Doubles 100,000—200,000 lire.

OPTIONS The **Museo dell'Ulivo** (Olive Museum) in Oneglia (9G) is sponsored by Carli, the region's largest oil maker. Displays include old olive presses and tools used over the centuries. To tour the vast olive-production region, take an intensive tasting-and-driving tour into the hills behind Imperia, up the Impero Valley through Pontedassio to the Colle di Nava, then west and down the Argentina Valley through Badalucco and Taggia. In November 2000, floods and mudslides damaged some olive groves, terraces, bridges, and roads behind Imperia, but at press time repairs and replantation were well under way.

RIVIERA DI PONENTE HIGHLIGHTS

After stately Bordighera, **San Remo** (8H) is the most popular port/resort on the Riviera dei Fiori. Though the inner sanctum of its Old Town is marginally menacing, a network of pedestrian streets just below holds a world of butchers, bakers, and Ligurian culinary boutiques. Grand 19th-century hotels and ancient, towering palm trees line the boulevards, and the casino retains its Old World glamour. The coastal highway between San Remo and Imperia offers occasional glimpses of the old, unspoiled Riviera before the plague of contemporary overbuilding struck. Just east of San Remo, the hill town of **Bussana Vecchia** (9G–H) was heavily damaged by a 19th-century earthquake; bohemian artists have colonized (and buttressed) the picturesque ruins. The beaches of the Ponente region are jam-packed with urban, commercial, sociable beach clubs, where families rent lounge chairs and umbrellas by the day, week, or month and spend the day sunning, playing cards, and visiting with fellow habitués.

RIVIERA DI LEVANTE

This is the second and wilder of the two Italian Rivieras. Spanning southeast from Genoa to Cinque Terre and the Golfo di La Spezia, the lower Ligurian coastline grows less developed and more isolated, with green cliffs dropping sharply down to the sea. The commercial beaches of the Ponente give way to rocky, rugged bays and inlets, and the most desirable resorts require some planning to get to. Between the yacht havens off the Portofino peninsula and the long-isolated Cinque Terre cliff villages there stretches a serpentine, tunnel-riddled autostrada that separates the misty, scarcely populated Alpine countryside from the sea.

ALBERGO DA GIOVANNI, SAN FRUTTUOSO (14E)
After the Last Boat Leaves, p. 56

While it can be overwhelmed by boatloads of day-trippers to its abbey and its fingernail of a pebble beach, this tiny, hill-framed inlet feels miles — and aeons — away from civilization once the ferries retreat. Access it on foot from Portofino or by ferry out of Portofino or Camogli. The inn has only seven simple (read: linoleum and laminate) rooms, each with screened windows overlooking the beach and bay. Each room has a sink and bidet; the two shared showers and toilets are up two flights. Half-pension and à la carte lunch and dinner are served on the balcony, with boat-fresh *frutti di mare* and fish presented whole (you select the preparation — grilled or oven-sauced).

CONTACT Albergo/Ristorante da Giovanni, Casella Postale 23, 15032 San Fruttuoso — Camogli (Genova), tel./fax 0185/770047.

DISTANCES Half-hour ferry ride from the Old Town port at Camogli, which is 25 km east of Genoa via Recco exit off A12.

PRICES Double rooms 100,000 — 140,000 lire; half board 160,000 — 170,000 lire per person.

OPTIONS To get a real sense of the abbey's isolation, hike over the forested hills high above the sea from San Fruttuoso to Portofino, passing ancient terraced farms and jungle-thick olive groves. Allow two to three hours.

HOTEL SPLENDIDO, PORTOFINO (14E)
La Dolce Vita, p. 8

Photogenic little Portofino is a veritable film set of a Mediterranean port, its ocher row houses curving in a near-perfect convex semicircle around the tiny harbor. Upscale boutiques cater to a yachting crowd, and open-air cafés and trattorias surround around the square that fronts the water. Hovering regal and aloof, this landmark hotel pampers an elite clientele with stunning views over the water from flower-draped balustrades. Boat and land excursions are easily arranged. 69 rooms. Restaurant, piano bar, pool bar, air-conditioning, pool, hair salon, sauna, gym, tennis court. Doubles 1,400,000 — 1,750,000 lire; full-board supplement 115,000 lire per person per day. Open April — mid-November.

CONTACT Hotel Splendido, Salita Baratta 16, 16034 Portofino, Genova, tel. 0185/267801, fax 0185/267806. www.orient-expresshotels.com. E-mail: reservations@splendido.net.

DISTANCES 38 km southeast of Genova via Rapallo—Santa Margherita exit from A12.

OPTIONS To be in the thick of things on the picturesque port, consider the sister hotel **Splendido Mare,** which offers a portside terrace restaurant and access to all Hotel Splendido facilities. Via Roma 2, 16034 Portofino, Genova, tel. 0185/267802, fax 0185/267807. www.orient-express hotels.com. E-mail: reservations@splendido.net. 16 rooms. 2 restaurants, piano bar, air-conditioning. Doubles 880,000—1,100,000 lire.

THE COASTAL TRAIL, CINQUE TERRE (16F)
Five Lands on Two Feet, p. 72

A series of five tiny cliff-villages that cling above the sea just northwest of La Spezia, the Cinque Terre were long inaccessible to the outside world except by terraced footpaths and small boats. The railroad first linked them in the early 20th century. Narrow, serpentine roads now connect the dots but require an investment of time and patience. By far the easiest way to visit the villages is to combine legwork with ferry and rail connections; boats give you a panoramic overview of the villages' cliff-bound settings, and trains can rumble you back to your lodging. The popular trail that laces up green cliffs and snakes into (and out of) each village often breaks out of dense olive and grape plantations into panoramic viewpoints, all part of Cinque Terre National Park. **Monterosso** is the most accessible and therefore the largest village, with a broad swath of beach and an Old Town well equipped for vacationers as well as short-term sightseers. There's a sociable night scene of open-air restaurants and *gelaterie* along the waterfront. **Vernazza** is often voted the most charming of the five, thanks to its Old Town and its pocket-size port surrounded by wave-washed rocks. **Corniglia** perches high above the water and has no port; its center consists of one narrow alley with a handful of cafés and restaurants. Just south of Corniglia, a sweep of steep stairs leads down to the train station and, below that, a long expanse of isolated stony beach. **Manarola** nestles on a steep hill above a miniature port and fishing cove lined with restaurants and bars. A mere half hour's stroll carries hikers over the paved and partially sheltered lovers' lane, known as the Via dell'Amore for its romantic sunset views. At the *via*'s far end lies **Riomaggiore,** the lively, popular entry village easily accessed from La Spezia and adopted, of late, by crowds of sociable students and twentysomething budget travelers, who mingle in the bars and *pensiones*. Whichever village you choose as a base, take the time to explore a few and settle into their quiet rhythm, as there is little to visit and a lot to be gained by finding a rocky perch and meditating on the ancient symbiosis between man and *mare.*

CONTACT Consorzio Turistico Cinqueterre, Piazza Garibaldi 29, Monterosso al Mare, La Spezia, tel. 0187/518341, fax 0187/523288. www.cinqueterre.it.

DISTANCES Riomaggiore lies 10 km west of greater La Spezia. Heading west from Riomaggiore, you reach Manarola after 1½ km, Corniglia after 3 more km, Vernazza after 3 more km, and Monterosso after 3½ more km. In the other direction, Monterosso is 12 km east of Levanto.

LODGING The handiest base for hiking the Cinque Terre trail and returning by train or boat is the beach resort of Monterosso. The stylish little **Hotel Villa Steno** stands apart on a hill above the Old Town, surrounded by lemon trees. Several of the sleek, modern rooms have idyllic private garden terraces looking over the Old Town to the sea. Via Roma 109, 19016 Monterosso al Mare, La Spezia, Cinque Terre, tel. 0187/817028, fax 0187/817354. www. pasini.com. Email: steno@pasini.com.

OPTIONS If you're athletically challenged, or simply in a *far niente* mood, drift, rather than hike, along the coastline in the scenic **ferry** cruiser that stops at four of the five villages and continues on to Portovenere (*see* Poets' Gulf, *below*). Contact Navigazione Golfo dei Poeti/Ligure Tirrena, tel. 0335/724—5221, fax 0187/730336.

CINQUE TERRE GRAPE HARVEST, GROPPO (16F)
Vineyard Vertigo, p. 34

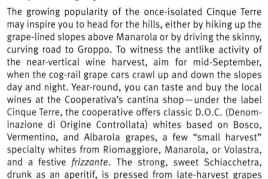

The growing popularity of the once-isolated Cinque Terre may inspire you to head for the hills, either by hiking up the grape-lined slopes above Manarola or by driving the skinny, curving road to Groppo. To witness the antlike activity of the near-vertical wine harvest, aim for mid-September, when the cog-rail grape cars crawl up and down the slopes day and night. Year-round, you can taste and buy the local wines at the Cooperativa's cantina shop—under the label Cinque Terre, the cooperative offers classic D.O.C. (Denominazione di Origine Controllata) whites based on Bosco, Vermentino, and Albarola grapes, a few "small harvest" specialty whites from Riomaggiore, Manarola, or Volastra, and a festive *frizzante*. The strong, sweet Schiacchetra, drunk as an aperitif, is pressed from late-harvest grapes and aged in oak. A selection of grappas and a southern-style *limoncino* (lemon liqueur) complete the line, which is made from the produce of a mere 80 hectares. In the old days some 500 hectares of vineyards plunged straight down to the sea, but they've been encroached on by tourism...and the vineyard heirs prefer to develop hotels these days.

CONTACT Cooperativa Agricoltura de Riomaggiore, Manarola, Corniglia, Vernazza e Monterosso, 19010 Loc. Groppo di Riomaggiore, La Spezia, tel. 0187/920435, fax 0187/920076. www.cantinacinqueterre.com. E-mail: coop5terre@cantina cinqueterre.com.

DISTANCES The cooperative sits 2 km above Riomaggiore, just southeast of Groppo.

LODGING Base yourself in the **Hotel Villa Argentina,** high above the Old Town in Riomaggiore. Nine of the cool, modern rooms have balconies that face the sea. Via de Gasperi 37, 19017 Riomaggiore, La Spezia, tel./fax 0187/920213. 15 rooms.

OPTIONS Liguria is known for its flavor-intensive specialties, marketed in pretty little jars and bottles under the blanket rubric *prodotti tipici* (*see* Olive Harvest, *above*). The best-known such product is pesto, once hand-ground from the wild basil that covered the green hills behind the sea. In addition to the well-known green, it comes in a red version, with sweet red peppers pestled in. Look also for dried tomato sauce, anchovy and olive pastes, fine, firm tuna bottled in extra-virgin oil, and, of course, tiny black olives preserved in brine. Take them home to flavor meat, fish, or fresh pasta...or buy a bag of *grissini* (breadsticks) and dip right in.

POETS' GULF, FROM PORTO VENERE TO TELLARO (17F)
Inciting the Extraordinary, p. 60

The Gulf of La Spezia, a broad, sheltered bay jutting into the Ligurian coastline, is better known as *il golfo dei poeti,* the Poets' Gulf. Its waters churning around black rock and pebble shores, its key towns craggy with ruined castles, its row houses glowing in tones of ocher, this is indeed a romantic and inspiring area—despite the modern tourism that has replaced the savage beauty sung by Byron and Shelley. La Spezia itself is a sprawling industrial city with a massive naval port; military helicopters and sea planes often roar overhead. But find a quiet corner—a back street, a pine-shaded rock, a chunk of Romanesque rampart overlooking the seething sea—and it's easy to call forth the poets' muse. Porto Venere anchors the western peninsula that shelters the gulf, and its watercolor-pretty harbor embodies the epic best of the gulf—rows of arcaded ocher houses, stacks of primary-color fishing boats, narrow backstreets leading up ramparts to a church and two ruined castles. Just below the ramparts, a plaque marks Byron's Grotto, from whence the poet is said to have swum to San Terenzo to pop in on the Shelleys. San Terenzo–Lerici is a busy family beach resort short on romance, but Lerici itself still blends palm-lined promenades, a posh pleasure port, and a dark-visaged castle that looms poetically over the yachts. Just up the road, the beach hamlet of Fiascherino was the chosen hideaway of D. H. Lawrence, who holed up with his lover in a stone blockhouse overlooking a rocky, isolated cove. In the old fishing village of Tellaro, a stone's throw up the road, Lawrence wandered the deep-pitched stone streets that spill into the tiny net-lined port.

CONTACT Azienda di Promozione Turistica Cinque Terre/Golfo dei Poeti, Viale Mazzini 47, 19200 La Spezia, tel. 0187/770900, fax 0187/770908. www.itsyn.it/apt/golfo _en.html.

DISTANCES Portovenere is 12 km south of La Spezia; Lerici is 12 km southeast, on the other side of the bay. Fiascherino lies 4 km southeast of Lerici, with Tellaro a kilometer farther.

LODGING To achieve maximum isolation and writerly inspiration, stay at pretty little **Locanda Il Senatore** in Fiascherino, perched between two beach coves looking toward the open sea. One of the two private beach areas abuts Lawrence's hideaway. Rooms look over the water, as does the broad, panoramic all-seafood restaurant, and there are full beach facilities (parasols, lounge chairs, bar service). Via Byron 11, Fiascherino di Lerici, La Spezia, tel. 0187/967236. Restaurant, bar, private beach. 14 rooms. Doubles 200,000 lire; with full board and beach facilities, 220,000 per person.

OPTIONS The Navigazione Golfo dei Poeti (Via Mazzini 21, 19121 La Spezia, tel. 0187/732987, www.navigazione golfodeipoeti.it) traces Byron's swim with all the comforts of a **cruise boat** between Porto Venere and Lerici. The cruise also circles the neighboring islands of Palmaria, Tino, and Tinetto, riddled with grottos and caves.

RIVIERA DI LEVANTE HIGHLIGHTS
With roads along the coast limited and often tangled, one of the best ways to tour the Levante **waterfront** is by sailboat or, if you're lucky, yacht. Hence each of the region's ports of call—Portofino, Rapallo, Cinque Terre, Portovenere, Lerici— shelter well equipped harbors and marinas. Cruise boats taxi the shoreline (*see above*), and on all but the stormiest days the coastal waters are crisscrossed with the wakes of speedboats and sails. Beaches can be soft and sandy, with plenty of basking-rocks all along the cliff-lined shore.

Having commuted from Lorraine to the south of France on a regular basis for her last Fodor's projects, *Fodor's Provence and the Côte d'Azur* and *Escape to Provence*, Nancy Coons expanded her research travels to include the Italian coast for *Escape to the Riviera.* First-hand adventures included boating 60 km out to sea with the Monaco oceanography team, riding a jeep into the inaccessible Vallée des Merveilles in the Mercantour National Park, and hiking the steep seaside trail that links the "five lands" of Cinque Terre. When she is not escaping for Fodor's she lives in a three-hundred-year-old farmhouse north of Metz, from where she has published pieces in the *Wall Street Journal, National Geographic Traveler, Opera News,* and *European Travel & Life.* When French school vacations allow (which is often), her husband Mark Olson and their daughters Elodie and Alice accompany her on the road. Even this can pall: After months of Riviera cuisine, Alice threatened "pesto-cide."

Owen Franken loves to cook and to eat. He traveled to Paris in 1988 for the food and wine, and decided to stay when he met a stunning blonde while standing in line at the bank. His work is now specialized in this domain (food and wine, not blondes). His photography has illustrated the pages of *Saveur, Gourmet, Bon Appetit, Food and Wine, Travel and Leisure, National Geographic, Forbes, Business Week,* the *New York Times* Dining, Travel, and Business sections, and many other clients worldwide. Having photographed Fodor's *Escape to Provence* and produced a photographic book of Spain, Franken is presently shooting the photographs for Patricia Wells's forthcoming *Paris Cookbook.* His work can be seen in cyberspace at www.francefoodtravelphotos.com.